THE BIZ

50 little things that make a big difference to team motivation and leadership

DAVID FREEMANTLE

NICHOLAS BREALEY
PUBLISHING

LONDON   BOSTON

First published by
Nicholas Brealey Publishing in 2004

3–5 Spafield Street
Clerkenwell, London
ECIR 4QB, UK
Tel: +44 (0)20 7239 0360
Fax: +44 (0)20 7239 0370

100 City Hall Plaza, Suite 501
Boston
MA 02108, USA
Tel: (888) BREALEY
Fax: (617) 523 3708

http://www.nbrealey-books.com
http://www.bizandbuzz.co.uk

ISBN 1-85788-346-2

British Library Cataloguing in Publication Data
A catalogue record for this book is available from the
British Library

Printed in Finland by WS Bookwell.

THE
BIZ

Also by David Freemantle and published by Nicholas Brealey:

The Buzz
50 little things that make a big difference
to delivering world-class customer service

and

What Customers Like About You
Adding emotional value for service excellence
and competitive advantage

CONTENTS

ACKNOWLEDGMENTS

Writing a book is rarely a smooth process in which a solitary author produces a perfect typescript for automatic conversion into the perfect book. More often the end product has been improved substantially as a result of inputs from a number of team players who work behind the scenes to advise, cajole, and encourage the author to make changes for the better. It can be a difficult process and I must confess I am not the easiest author to deal with in this connection. It is easy to give advice but not to take it.

I thought I had written the perfect book until Nicholas Brealey, my publisher whose patience I must have exhausted, came along and struggled to convince me—the stubborn and difficult author—that the book could be even better. On reflection, he was absolutely right. I am duly indebted to Nicholas along with his excellent support team in the form of Victoria Bullock, Angie Tainsh, and Sally Lansdell for their helpful inputs and their forbearance in dealing with me.

My wife Mechi, as on many occasions previously, has been incredibly supportive during my extended absences at home and abroad while I researched and wrote this book (and its companion). She also made many helpful suggestions with regard to the text. I am duly grateful.

However, the prime inspiration for this book comes from the many "star performers" I have had the privilege of meeting around the world over recent times. These range from employees who have excelled in their performance at the front line to highly motivational chief executives who have a "switched-on," people-oriented and customer-focused approach that delivers results. Many of these people are mentioned by name in this book and I would like to thank each one of them for their inspiration.

INTRODUCTION

Doing the biz

*"As a racing driver, I trained myself to deal with each corner at a time.
You can't jump ahead. Everything is achieved by inches."*
Damon Hill, Formula One World Champion, 1996

The best team leaders do the biz. They make a difference. They motivate their people to perform exceptionally well and achieve the required results on a daily basis as well as in the longer term.

These bosses understand what the biz is all about and so do their teams. They are focused and they have flair. They have the energy and they have the edge. Furthermore, they have fun when they are fighting hard to deliver the goods. That's the biz. It's all about delivering and making things happen—for customers, for team members, for the company, and of course for themselves.

The biz is not simply a matter of implementing grand strategies and pursuing long-term visions. Nor does it involve intellectual debate about the values to be applied in the way the organization is managed and customers are handled.

The biz *is* a matter of daily operations, of the little things that the best bosses do and think on a minute-by-minute basis that have such a big impact on the teams they manage.

The best team leaders do the biz when they step through the door at 8.00 a.m. on a Monday morning. That's because they choose to step through that door at 8.00 a.m. as opposed to 9.00 or 10.00. Every little choice they make, even what time they start work, will be observed and will have a big impact on the team's motivation.

Thus the decision of what to do first—whether to pick up the phone, check the email, read a newspaper, grab a coffee, go and see the director, chat to the secretary, or walk around saying "Hi!" to every team member and asking about their weekend—will have an impact.

The worst bosses get these small behaviors wrong and the best bosses excel at them. That's the biz.

There is no theory behind the biz, any more than there can be a theory behind marriage. So this book is not full of theory, let alone grand stratagems. Instead, it is full of the little things that we can choose to think and do that will make a big difference in the way we motivate our teams.

One key premise

However, there is one premise that is important: motivated people perform more effectively in delivering results than demotivated people. This is almost a truism, but even so it is worth stating because it begs the corollary that to achieve results a boss must concentrate on motivation. It is amazing how many companies and managers ignore this simple premise.

PUTTING PEOPLE FIRST

My first management job was as a Production Manager with the American chocolate manufacturer Mars Ltd. It was then and still is an excellent company. I learnt many valuable management lessons at Mars and one of them was that to excel in business you have to invest an inordinate amount of time, energy, and effort in getting the people thing right. That principle has stayed with me throughout my career, which included a post on the board of an airline. With the hindsight of wisdom and all my experiences with a multitude of companies around the world, some good and some not so good, I still believe in this principle. If you don't focus your management energies on people, then they won't focus their energies on the company.

Despite the proliferation of personnel and HR departments (which might be part of the problem), the Mars approach is rare. It is all too common to visit companies and find demoralized people who moan and groan about their big bad bosses. These employees don't feel valued and complain that their bosses walk all over them, demand too much from them, and give too little in return. That is one reason an increasing number of professional people have given up their careers in large companies to go and live in the countryside, on lower incomes, and take up new interests there. While most people accept the premise that to be successful in management you must put people first, it is all too clear from a growing number of reports and newspaper cases that this rarely happens. In their pursuit of short-term profit, too many managers neglect the essential people factor in the business equation.

Choosing positive behaviors

This means choosing positive behaviors and attitudes that will maximize the chance of stimulating other people's positive motivational choices. Thus if your team leader shouts loudly at you and rebukes you when something has gone wrong, you have a choice. You can choose to be demotivated (by getting defensive and becoming negative) or you can choose to be motivated (by learning the lessons and applying them). Equally, the team leader has a choice too. He or she can choose *not* to rebuke you and instead choose to counsel you. In doing so, he or she chooses an attitude, whether it is to hurt you with a rebuke—hoping that this will motivate you to learn—or to demonstrate some positive support with the offer of counseling—thus also motivating you to learn. All bosses make these minute-by-minute behavioral choices every day and they can have a big impact on morale. When bosses make effective choices they are doing the biz—they achieve the desired results because the people in their teams are motivated to do so.

About this book

This book focuses on these choices, on the people factor and the biz mindset. It highlights many of the little things a successful boss has to do. It is aimed at any boss who needs to motivate other people on a daily basis. This could be a team leader in a bank, a department manager in a retail store, a middle manager in a government agency or a charity. It could be a foreman on a building site or a supervisor in a call center. It could be a manager working in IT or a graduate trainee aspiring to promotion.

Confucius said, "A journey of a thousand miles starts with the first step." This book is about all the little steps necessary to do the biz.

I suggest you read this book a section a day, focusing each day on one simple step (specified at the end of that section) that you can take with respect to your behavior or attitude in doing the biz. Each of these little behaviors and attitudes is easy to apply. By concentrating on one such behavior or thought each day, you will begin to build up a reputation as a great boss who motivates people and who actually does the biz.

The book can also be used for those invaluable half-hour team sessions that many companies and their managers hold on a daily or weekly basis. One idea is to put onto the agenda of each team session: "Feedback—what can I do better as boss? For example, should I be doing (more of) this type of thing..." (then referring to one section from this book).

Another application that will prove helpful to in-house trainers is to develop a series of training modules using selected sections from the book.

Finally, as it is impossible to separate employee motivation from customer motivation (the two go together), I suggest readers also dip into the companion volume entitled *The Buzz: 50 little things that make a big difference to delivering world-class customer service*.

I guarantee that if you practice the various steps specified in this book on a daily basis, over a period of 10 weeks (50 working days), then you will have such a motivated team of people that you will do the biz and achieve the results you want for your organization.

Forward to the basics...!

THE PREMIER DIVISION

A great boss will tell you, "It's all about people." A bad boss will say, "It's all about money."

As Confucius said, "The gold in your heart is more precious than the gold in your purse." The best team leaders devote their working lives to helping people discover the gold in their hearts and allowing it to shine on others. We all become richer that way.

There are 12 little things that the best team leaders do in getting started on doing the biz. These make up the premier division of essential behaviors for team leadership and motivation. If you practice these, you will be well on the road to having a high-performing team.

1	**Make people your top priority**
2	**Be an exemplar**
3	**Give cause (aspire)**
4	**Hire the best**
5	**Fight to pay the best**
6	**Personalize relationships**
7	**Liberate people with trust**
8	**Communicate immediately**
9	**Initiate learning**
10	**Know what you want to be**
11	**Agree the contribution to be made**
12	**Measure what is important**

MAKE PEOPLE YOUR TOP PRIORITY

Always put your people first in allocating your time and deciding on your agenda.

The most important little thing you can do is give time to your people and thus demonstrate that they have top priority. The odd minute, the half-hour chat, and the occasional relaxed hour with them are critical if you are going to motivate people to do the biz.

Giving top priority to team members requires you to drop everything for them in times of need. Nothing is more important for the biz. Furthermore, in order for you to motivate team members they need to know the value you place on them and how critical you see their contribution as being. They need to know that their team leader is interested in their work and would rather devote time to supporting them than doing other things.

78 high-priority minutes

- One minute looking at Fernando's new car.
- Two minutes joking with Eddie about the football.
- Three minutes hearing about Jamil's sister's wedding.
- Four minutes reviewing with Ayshath her project report.
- Five minutes listening to Andrew's account of his meeting.
- Six minutes advising Carlton on his budget figures and plans.
- Seven minutes congratulating Mercedes on her sales success.
- Eight minutes counseling Colette on her relationship problems.
- Nine minutes discussing Jackie's proposed update for the website.
- Ten minutes with Ann helping her rehearse a presentation to the CEO.
- Eleven minutes' follow-up with Beatrice concerning her transfer request.
- Twelve minutes on a team meeting to update people on last week's results.

When team leaders fail to find time for people and assign them low priority, those people begin to feel neglected and make assumptions that their leaders don't care and are not interested in their work or problems. While no boss can be on site every day, it is essential that you set time aside in your diary for wandering around and chatting to people. A boss's diary should never be so full that there is no time for other people.

The intention of giving high priority to spending time with team members is not to communicate key messages but to learn what is going on in people's lives and at work. Excellent team leaders will be keen to learn what has been happening in employees' day-to-day routines: the exceptions, the problems, the successes, and the stories. They will want to increase their understanding of people's work situations and their specific needs, whether it be addressing a problem with a malfunctioning piece of equipment or dealing with an issue relating to a particularly troublesome customer. In this way leaders can assign top priority to helping team members resolve their problems at work.

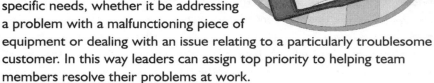

When an issue does arise they will stop at nothing to get it resolved. Where appropriate they will chase head office for a resolution. They will also ensure that people issues are at the top of the agenda for meetings with their own senior executive and the head office team. The last thing these bosses will do is allow issues to fester.

To prevent this happening, good team leaders will assign a high priority to sitting down with each team member for a regular informal chat about "the story so far." They will update individuals and the team on progress and demonstrate the importance they are giving to getting specific problems resolved.

On the rare occasions when a big issue blows up or an incident occurs, these bosses will drop everything to help their team. They will walk out of meetings, cancel travel plans, and automatically place the highest emphasis on joining the team to help them solve the problem.

THE BIZ STEP 1
Ask your team straight: Do I assign a sufficiently high priority to providing the support you need?

BIZ POINT

A reflection of what you value in life is not how you spend your money, but how you spend your time and the priorities you set.

7

2 BE AN EXEMPLAR

Set the best example with every little thing you do and say.

Every little thing you do has a positive, negative, or neutral impact on your team's motivation. There is no avoiding it. As a boss you are under observation all the time—even when people can't see you. In fact, those bosses who are rarely seen are the worst examples of all, failing to support the team in times of need. Not that you have to be there all the time interfering with everything going on—that would be a bad example too.

You set the standard of behavior that the team will emulate. It is the same with values. They don't need to be written down or even debated at length—your values are reflected in everything you do and as such are an example of the values that your team will strive to adopt and exceed to please you.

The best team leaders are exemplars of:
- ✔ Punctuality (they are always on time).
- ✔ Volunteering (they offer to help when the workload is high).
- ✔ Charm (they are hospitable and welcome all visitors warmly).
- ✔ Openness and honesty (they are completely trusted by everyone).
- ✔ Courtesy (they always treat others with respect and are well-mannered).
- ✔ Equality (they fetch the tea for everyone and treat everyone the same).
- ✔ Listening (they are not opinionated and will give full attention to what people say).
- ✔ Hard work (they never skive off or take it easy when the team is hard-pressed).
- ✔ Positive thinking (they are never negative, never complain or speak badly of others).
- ✔ Precision in paperwork (they make few mistakes, their facts and figures are perfect, and their presentation is excellent).
- ✔ Decisiveness (they know how to make decisions and when to leave a decision to the team).

Team leaders are living examples of the expectations to be exceeded, of the excellence to be adopted, of the imperfections to be forgiven and the lessons to be learnt. The way bosses talk to customers will set a standard by which their team will judge them. If their standards are low, the example will be bad and the team will judge them accordingly. If their standards are high, the team will attempt to emulate their practice of excellence. This applies equally to the concisely written word, the prompt response to emails, the warm tone adopted in taking a call, and the clarity of presentations.

The way team leaders speak to team members is an example of the way they think and feel about their team. It is an example of their own personality.

The example bosses set should never be static, to be repeated day in and day out. Like any good thing it can be improved on by pushing back the boundaries. There is always a better way and excellent team leaders set an example by striving to find the best approach to be adopted and followed. There might just be a better way of engaging customers, of communicating with suppliers, of behaving with the board, of inspiring the team, and of spending time. Leaders are always in pursuit of the best.

What are the high standards that you exemplify at work?

Encouragement, celebration, praise, punishment, and the odd remark and scathing comment are all aspects that can either enthuse or infect a team. Motivation is a product of the minutest of examples set by bosses first thing on a Monday morning and last thing on a Friday evening. It is a product of who team leaders speak to (and who they don't) and what they do throughout the week.

The emperor might wear no clothes, but the people will see him for what he is—and that is the standard for good or bad by which judgments about the boss are made. There is no escaping everyday reality. The example cannot be written down. It has to be practiced—in fact, it is everything practiced by team leaders.

THE BIZ STEP 2
Become conscious every day of the example you set and then set out to become an exemplar of all that is best in your business. That's the biz.

BIZ POINT
As a boss you are an exemplar whether you like it or not. The question is: Do you exemplify the best?

2

9

3 GIVE CAUSE (ASPIRE)

Give cause to everything you and the team do.
Aspiration is the source of all motivation.

One little thing effective team leaders need to do is to clarify where they are taking the business in the medium to long term. The fashionable word for this is "vision" (termed "biz vis" in this book).

Two other ways of expressing the "biz vis" are "cause" and "aspiration." An effective business has a leadership cause together with an aspiration to achieve it. The two are linked, as it takes spirit to pursue a cause. It thus becomes our aspiration (a word that relates to the direction of the spirit). Nelson Mandela had both an aspiration and a cause: to end apartheid and unify South Africa. It motivated a whole nation—now they

are doing the biz and the economy is growing. Walt Disney had an aspiration and a cause: to create happiness through fun characters, films, cartoons, and theme parks. Everyone can relate to these causes because they relate to their own personal beliefs and aspirations about the best way forward for today, tomorrow, and next year. The belief (in the cause) and the aspiration are vested in a person's soul and stimulate the spiritual energies that drive behavior.

All the little things team leaders say and do should reflect the aspirational cause they hold for the business. When this is articulated in a simple and meaningful way, people can identify with it. This will spark their own spirit and motivational energies to support and contribute in moving toward the biz vis.

The word "because" is useful here as it leads us to what will "be" the "cause." Thus a good test for finding the source of motivation is to complete the sentence: "We do this because…" If the completed statement is clear, succinct, and acceptable, the probability is that the team leader has a good cause that will encourage the team's spiritual and emotional energies to move forward.

Cause is related to reason, motivation, and answering the question: "Why do we do this?" For example, you might ask: "Why are our absentee levels increasing?" The word "because" will lead you to the answer.

A study of any well-known leader will reveal a cause. Churchill had a cause (so did Hitler, for that matter). Jack Welch had a cause: to be number one in each of General Electric's business segments. Michael Dell had a cause: to find a better way of making and distributing computers and thus reduce their price for customers. In the 1980s Sir Colin Marshall's cause for British Airways was for it to become the world's favorite airline.

However, the cause cannot be created only by the icons at the top of the organization. While a high-level strategic cause is essential, there needs to be an operational cause for every team leader—and every individual. In a perfect world all three causes (strategic, team, and individual) should be intrinsically interwoven.

Examples of a team leader's operational cause might be:

- ✪ As a team we will buzz because we want every customer to be satisfied with what we do for them.
- ✪ As a call center we will respond efficiently, effectively, and with empathy to our customers because we want every customer to have a good memory of us.
- ✪ As a team of technicians we will develop our expertise because we want our customers' problems to be fixed quickly and finally.
- ✪ As a team of engineers we are going to work flat out this weekend because we want this technical problem to be solved.
- ✪ As a sales team we are going to improve our approach to customers because we need to generate more revenue.

THE BIZ STEP 3

Take one little step today and clarify your team's cause. Keep asking yourself and the team: "Why?" and "Why do we do this?"

Use the word "because" to help you provide an answer. If you cannot believe in the answer and it does not align with your aspiration, then reconsider your work and your approach to it.

BIZ POINT

Ideally, the soul of an individual, of a team, and of an organization should be centered on a cause (the belief and the aspiration). That's the biz vis.

4 HIRE THE BEST

The best people to hire are those who are motivated to be the best in their chosen field.

The biz starts at the beginning: unless you hire the best people you will be in trouble for many months if not years to come. When you hire

second- or third-rate people you lock yourself into performance troubles and you will waste time trying to extricate the company from all the problems that these laggards create. Poor performers are time wasters. They waste everyone's time with the problems they cause.

When you hire people, one little thing you should do that will make a big difference is to look for their motivation. This will be reflected in:

The best track record	The candidate is motivated to achieve great results.
The best skills/talents	The candidate has a high degree of self-awareness and is motivated to focus on and develop what he or she is best at in life and at work.
The best experience	The candidate is motivated to develop his or her career by gaining new experiences.
The best knowledge	The candidate is motivated to learn and become an expert in his or her chosen field.
The best behavior	The candidate is motivated to create the best personal approach.
The best relationship skills	The candidate is motivated to work well with people.
The best potential	The candidate is ambitious and is motivated to do even better than in the past.
The best energy levels	The candidate is motivated to work hard to achieve personal goals at work.
The best attitude	The candidate is motivated to be positive, helpful, and a good team member.
The best imagination	The candidate is motivated to find creative ways of overcoming problems and creating a bright new future for the team and the company.
The best qualifications	The candidate is motivated to demonstrate formally, through qualifications, that he or she is exceptionally well educated.

| The best employers | The candidate is motivated to work for only the best employers. |
| The best pay | The candidate sees pay as a barometer of success and therefore has always been paid the best. |

These factors apply whether you are hiring a chief executive or a bus driver. For example, it is far better to hire a bus driver who is motivated to have the best safety record and to learn about customer service than to hire a bus driver who is merely there to earn money by driving a bus from A to B.

It can often be a struggle to find the best. Even if the market is tight, this is no reason for selecting second best. There are many enlightened and progressive executives who, on encountering a person who is the best, will hire them irrespective of whether or not there is a job vacancy. When you find the best people, hire them immediately.

If you want to do the biz and the best for your employees, customers, company, and shareholders, then you have no option but to recruit the best people. Anyone else will drag the company down.

This means that for every little step of the way in the recruitment and selection process, you have to qualify each decision with the word "best"—the best advertisement, the best selection methodology, the best interviewers, and the best candidates.

THE BIZ STEP 4
When it is time to fill the next job vacancy, apply the word "best" to the first step in the process and every step thereafter.

BIZ POINT
Your company can only be as good as the people you recruit.

5 FIGHT TO PAY THE BEST

If someone leaves your employ for better pay, you have failed. If you don't pay the best, someone else will and you won't be the best.

The underpinning philosophy of all the practices specified in this book is that for your team members to do the best, the team leader has to do the best for them. An intrinsic part of doing the best relates to pay. One little but very important thing you can do for your team is to fight to get them the best pay possible within the budgetary constraints of the business.

People are not commodities to be traded on the shopfloor for the lowest possible price. As a strategic policy the pursuit of the cheapest source of labor is a policy that will bring disaster to a company in the long term.

An assertion such as "people are our greatest asset" is meaningless unless you take all the little steps necessary to pay the best. When times are tough and revenues decline, it is your best people who are going to get you out of the trough. If you drive these best people away by reducing their pay, you will be doomed.

The best people command the best pay and they will travel to wherever they can find it. Quality, motivation, and business performance will suffer as soon as people realize that they could be better off working elsewhere.

If you want the best for your customers and your company in a very competitive marketplace, there is no other logic than the following:

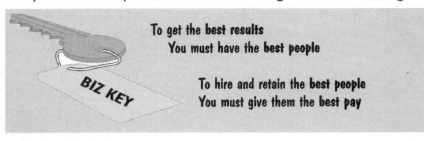

To get the best results
You must have the **best people**

To hire and retain the **best people**
You must give them the **best pay**

There is nothing new about this. There is an ancient adage of immense wisdom that states: "Pay peanuts, get monkeys."

Most people want the best for themselves, their families, and hopefully their communities. It is the prerogative of every employee—not of their employer—to determine what the best means to them.

Eight key motivational drivers for most people are that:

✪ They can feed their family.
✪ They have a roof over their head.
✪ Their children receive the best education possible.
✪ They are healthy and have the best medical provision when necessary.
✪ They can enjoy their leisure and vacation time with new stimuli.
✪ They do work that interests them and that they feel makes a contribution.
✪ They can improve themselves.
✪ They can do good for their community.

What is perceived to be the best is relative to the market and has to take into account other benefits that your employees value. However, in the end it is employees who decide what they believe is the best.

As a boss, therefore, you have no other option but to aim to be the best in the marketplace in paying your employees the best.

THE BIZ STEP 5

You cannot afford for any one of your employees to feel bad because of low pay. This puts the company at risk.

Find out now how your team members feel and take action to ensure that everyone is paid the best in the circumstances that prevail. Then ensure that your employees give of their best.

BIZ POINT
What you pay your shareholders is determined by what you pay your employees—the more the merrier in both cases.

6 PERSONALIZE RELATIONSHIPS

You cannot motivate your team unless you treat each individual as a human being. This means personalizing your relationship with each one.

You can call it whatever you like, employee relations or labor relations, but in the end it is all about relationships. Successful business is built on motivated relationships and one essential stream of relationships is between team leaders and their teams. When these fail the business stops. Where there is a trade union this means a strike and employees walk out. In a non-unionized company the same applies—when relationships fail employees walk away to work elsewhere.

To do the biz, team leaders need to discover a whole world of little personal things about each team member and thus build a relationship based on mutual personal interest. For example:

BEING PERSONAL

❖ How did Vijay's best friend's party go?
❖ What does Asha like to do at weekends?
❖ Has Lauren completed her studies yet?
❖ Has Edward's court case come up yet?
❖ How did Nancy's hospital visit go?
❖ How are Tariq's elderly parents?
❖ Why is Samuel looking so grim?
❖ What does Kesh really want?
❖ Why is Kenny so often annoyed?
❖ Where is Cheng Min going on vacation?

❖ What are Nora's interests outside work?
❖ When will Michael's graduation take place?
❖ What does Faye think of the latest blockbuster film?
❖ Can I see the photos of Gladys's grandchildren? Here are some photos of my kids.

Being personal is synonymous with treating each employee as a genuine human being. It means appreciating what makes them tick, what annoys them, what makes them feel good, and what makes them come to work every day. It means knowing something about their family as well as about their interests outside work. It means striving to understand the total person and doing your best to help that person accomplish his or her goals at work.

Did you know I'm a Libra too?

Being personal leads to a high degree of motivation. The converse, a totally impersonal approach, inevitably leads to demotivation. Furthermore, being personal is a two-way process that involves revealing some personal aspects about yourself to team members. This helps create the necessary emotional connections and demonstrates that you too are a human being with a heart.

Inevitably there are boundaries. Personalizing relationships with team members is not synonymous with becoming intimate or even close to them. What it means is discovering innocuous areas of common interest within which a personal relationship can be grounded and built.

One chief executive I knew who led a major financial institution would always take a written note of people's names and what key points they told him. The next time he visited the location he would check his notes beforehand, thus enabling him to recall the name of the receptionist, Christine, and that she had two daughters called Sophie and Debbie.

Personalizing relationships is easy. All you have to do is forget about work for a few minutes and remember that you are dealing with real people who have real interests outside work—and then make that personal connection.

THE BIZ STEP 6
Every day take one little step toward building personal relationships with your team members, for example by taking an interest in what they do outside work.

BIZ POINT

To win people's hearts and minds you have to create personal relationships with them. It is not intellectual but an emotional process that comes from your heart.

7 LIBERATE PEOPLE WITH TRUST

Remove the shackles and trust your people to get on and make all the necessary decisions.

People work best when they are liberated and enjoy a high degree of trust. There is a myth that trust has to be earned, that you start from a zero base and build up to a position of total trust depending on whether people behave in a trustworthy way. This is unrealistic and impractical. All it does is breed suspicion.

The Tao (The Way of the Ways) says: "When you are lacking in trust, others have no trust in you."

One little thing you need to do as a new team leader is to start with 100 percent trust in your team members. Unless you have evidence to the contrary, you should trust each of them to get on and do the job, making whatever decisions are necessary. There should be no need for them to come running to you every five minutes asking permission to step out of line or spend ten cents on a customer. In fact, there should be no need for you to give permission for anything other than major expenditure. Ideally, your team members should be empowered to choose their own working hours, their own times for meal breaks, as well as where to work, who to talk to, and generally how to go about their jobs. That is total liberation.

TRUST IN TEAM	
Trust	Distrust
100%	0
80%	20%
60%	40%
40%	60%
20%	80%
0	100%

**Do you have
X% TRUST or Y% DISTRUST
in your team?**

Henry Stewart, chief executive of Happy Computers, says: "Providing they operate within the principles of the company we give our people total freedom in the way they work." In Happy Computers people choose their own working hours and job titles and have many other freedoms.

Trust gives another person the freedom to act on your behalf. You are effectively assigning to another individual the power of attorney to make decisions for you. Trust is at the cornerstone of all teamwork. It liberates a group of people to exercise responsibility and operate in the best interests of the company. This is highly motivational.

Trusting people means refusing to make decisions for them. The more you make decisions for people, the more you are demonstrating your lack of trust in their capabilities. Assuming that you have trained them well they should have sufficient knowledge and experience to make their own decisions.

It is only when people betray your trust that you can conclude they are not trustworthy, not before.

The critical area relating to trust, liberation, and responsibility is money. A good test of how far you have gone down this route is to answer the question: "How much of the company's money can a front-line person spend without having to ask permission from a higher authority?" The larger the amount, the greater the freedom and trust you have in your organization.

Here are some other simple tests of liberation and trust:

Without permission from their bosses, can front-line people:
- ✔ Obtain a fresh supply of consumables?
- ✔ Choose their own working hours?
- ✔ Spend money on customers?
- ✔ Invest in a training course?
- ✔ Order new equipment?
- ✔ Work off-line?
- ✔ Entertain suppliers?
- ✔ Organize a celebration?
- ✔ Initiate changes in the working environment (e.g., move desks around)?

THE BIZ STEP 7
To demonstrate trust and liberation, review your expenditure sign-off limits.
Do your front-line people have sufficient authority to do their jobs effectively?

BIZ POINT
Trust is mutual. Before you can trust your team they have to trust you.

7

COMMUNICATE IMMEDIATELY

Inform people about the way things are and tell them now.

Immediacy is critical in communicating with team members when news breaks. People are motivated when they are the first to learn and demotivated when they are the last to find out.

There are a number of little things you can do to ensure that you communicate effectively with your people about what is going on in the company:

✔ Inform your team immediately you find out something significant. Make this a top priority.
✔ Tell them the facts without embellishing them.
✔ Use face-to-face communication wherever possible.
✔ If you have opinions about the facts, ensure your people know that these are your opinions.
✔ Use group communication wherever possible (thus avoiding repetition to a sequence of individuals).
✔ Where group communication is not possible, communicate concisely with each team member.
✔ Avoid emails and text messages. If a face-to-face conversation is not possible, talk on the phone. Emails and text messages should only be used as a last resort. They are the lazy way to communicate.
✔ Only inform people of things that they view as affecting them or that are of direct interest to them.
✔ When communicating with team members take them into your confidence. Trust them with confidential information.
✔ If the information really is confidential (and commercially sensitive), do not put it in writing. Keep the communication verbal.
✔ Drop everything else to keep your team informed. The best bosses ensure that there is plenty of blank space in their diaries for communication. Thus if they know they are attending a board meeting, they will set some blank time aside afterwards for debriefing the team.

People are naturally curious and often suspicious about what is going on in an organization, especially if they sense a change that is going to affect them. They will speculate, gossip, and perpetuate rumors. All this can be time wasting if not subversive. Overall it saps the organization's strength as people huddle in corners discussing half-truths and the latest hearsay. There is only one way to overcome this—to place top priority on communicating the facts immediately to as many people as possible.

The worst thing that can happen is for an employee to discover from a friend in another department a change affecting him or her, without being informed by the boss about it. This is a sure way to demotivate people. Absence of communication effectively devalues employees by sending the signal: "We have more important things to do than communicate with you about important changes."

Tell team members before communicating any news to the media and the rest of the world. This requires a high degree of sensitivity to and understanding of the team. A good team leader knows what sort of news the team should be informed about and what is of no interest to them at all.

One example of really bad communication was a man who left work on a Friday afternoon and was unable to get out of the car park because his security pass would not activate the barrier. He approached the security guard, who checked a list and told him he had been made redundant that afternoon. Therefore his pass had been deactivated. The man's team leader had not told him. Another true story is of an individual who was not told that his boss had left and that he was now reporting to a new manager—who also had not bothered to inform him.

Whatever the change, whatever the decision—no matter how big or small—it is imperative that employees are informed immediately, ideally face to face.

THE BIZ STEP 8
As a team leader set yourself a personal standard: "The first to know after me is my team—and that will be my top priority."

BIZ POINT

The only task a manager has is to communicate.

8

INITIATE LEARNING

Encourage learning, but don't insist on training.

It is said that you train a dog to bark and train a child to use the potty. Gardeners train plants to go up a trellis. Railway trains go along lines and if you want your people to go along the same lines you had better train them.

When it comes to the workplace, training is essential for a wide range of impersonal skills (such as keyboard skills, driving a forklift truck, or fixing computers), but inappropriate for personal skills (such as selling, customer relations, and leadership). You cannot train a couple to be happily married, but they can learn as they go along.

WHAT I LEARNT TODAY

✔ I learnt that happiness is a choice.
✔ I learnt that Jacksons, our competitor, is putting its prices up.
✔ I finally got to understand depreciation and how accountants calculate it.
✔ I discovered some new features on the ZETA+ software we recently installed.
✔ I found out what Hamish Buchanan actually does in his role as business development manager.

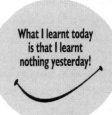

What I learnt today is that I learnt nothing yesterday!

✔ I learnt that we have run out of ITEMX and it is on back order, with delivery expected in three weeks.
✔ I learnt that Marjorie has a serious nut allergy and collapsed yesterday after eating donuts.
✔ I learnt that our customers aren't happy with waiting times and I can take action on this.
✔ I learnt that Ouagadougou is the capital of Burkina Faso and that we have an office there.
✔ I learnt about myself—some people think I'm too negative and complain too much.
✔ I learnt that our managing director speaks fluent Mandarin.
✔ I learnt about the revised conditions on our new warranty.
✔ I learnt how to spell Connecticut and the Philippines.
✔ I learnt that Rachna is pregnant with twins.

Training is all about programming people to acquire and apply a set of specified competences. The process is subconscious. Once people are trained, little thought is required for them to exercise the competency.

It virtually happens automatically. The skills acquired through training are normally tangible and can be measured.

Learning, in contrast, is all about motivation and self-improvement. It is never ending and does not merely relate to skills but also to the acquisition and application of knowledge, experience, and wisdom. When people are motivated to learn they take advantage of training as well as of many other learning opportunities. Conversely, when people are not motivated to learn, training will prove to be a waste of time.

The best bosses therefore do a lot of little things to encourage people to learn and to provide learning opportunities to help them. For example:

- ✪ They study new product literature with their staff.
- ✪ They assign people tasks that stretch them to learn.
- ✪ They run little quizzes and give prizes for the best scores.
- ✪ They bring in guest speakers for the occasional lunchtime session.
- ✪ They ensure that there are books, journals, and DVDs around to learn from.
- ✪ They highlight mistakes and convert these into vital learning opportunities.
- ✪ They devote half an hour every week to team learning on chosen topics.

Ideally a little learning should take place every day and the lessons should be brought into focus with a team member (or the boss) as the tutor.

An integral part of the learning process is to identify individual aspirations and help people meet these. Thus if an employee aspires to move from back office to front office, an enlightened boss can help by providing the necessary learning opportunities.

Team leaders who believe in the importance of personal development for their team will find a way to achieve it, budget or no budget, and to ensure it takes place.

THE BIZ STEP 9

Identify the aspirations of each member of your team for being better and doing better.

Then identify some learning opportunities to help each person realize their aspirations.

BIZ POINT

Humility is a key to learning. It is an awareness that there are always opportunities to be better and do better.

10 KNOW WHAT YOU WANT TO BE

Be true to what you want to be in everything you do with your team.

Every little thing you do at work should reflect the true you and what you want to be. You are the genuine article. If you try to be what someone else wants you to be, you will appear false and artificial. As soon as you start parroting other people's phrases and thoughts, you will be seen as a stooge, a yes-man, or a clone of the system. You will blow with the wind, run with the hares, and hunt with the hounds. You will become an organizational chameleon who colors their words differently every week depending on the prevailing fashion.

It is tough trying to be what you want to be. It forces you to know what you stand for and then to stand up for these convictions. It requires courage when expediency is an easier route. It means putting your head above the parapet and saying what you believe is right, when the safer route is to keep your head down and avoid being shot at.

Striving to be what you want to be gives you power to direct your behavior and communications so that people believe in you and know you mean what you do and say. In other words, you are always true to yourself.

LOOK AT YOURSELF
What am I?
What do I want to be?

THIS IS ME NOW	THIS IS HOW I WANT TO BE
Shy	Outgoing
Intelligent	Sought out for my intelligent help
A bit of a loner	Socially accepted by the team
Expert in my field	Highly respected for my expertise
Self-deprecating	Confident and appreciated by others
Low self-esteem	High self-esteem
A little selfish	Generous and giving
A little intolerant	More trusting and tolerant

You cannot be one thing one day and something else another day. You mean what you say and say what you mean. There should be no falseness about your approach, only genuineness. Nor should there be any hidden agendas or ulterior motives. You come clean because you are straight with people.

Being yourself requires a high degree of self-awareness, about your talents and limitations, your feelings and emotions, and how these relate to your principles, values, beliefs, and aspirations. When you know what you want to be, your own strengths and weaknesses become increasingly clear as you progress through life, because you are forever trying to enhance the former and limit the latter.

Bosses who can be themselves are very motivating, because people know exactly where they stand with them and what they are like. They can understand such bosses and relate to them without fear of volatility in mood or thought.

When you know yourself you are able to give of yourself. In doing so you reveal insights into your own heart and soul.

Your personal behavioral style effectively becomes a reflection of your true self. When you speak to team members and take an interest in them it is because you genuinely want to—not because a textbook or a training course insisted that you do so. When you present a small gift to someone, whether it be a candy or a word of praise, that person will know it is for real and not some psychological trick to curry favor.

Falseness, flattery, hypocrisy, two-facedness, and lip service are out of the question for team leaders who are true to themselves. What you get is the genuine article—that is being yourself.

THE BIZ STEP 10

Dig deep into your soul and ask yourself: Am I myself at work, or am I what someone else wants me to be? In other words, do I act out a role that does not reflect what I want to be? If you do, you will need to do something about it.

BIZ POINT
To motivate people you cannot be what someone else wants you to be. You have to be yourself.

AGREE THE CONTRIBUTION TO BE MADE

Avoid telling people what to think and what to do. Instead, agree the contribution to be made.

One of the simplest things a team leader can do is agree the contribution to be made by each team member and then allow them to get on and make it. The key word here is "agree." When you have people's agreement to an action they are more likely to do it. If you tell them to do it, by instruction or imposition, they will do it less well if they do it at all.

Agreement is more likely to be reached when there are good personal relationships within the team and there is a high degree of mutual understanding and respect. It does not take much to reach agreement other than the investment of some time and an exchange of views.

The "tell, tell, tell" culture is endemic in many organizations. It is prevalent in hierarchical companies where status is dominant and being task-driven is the normal mode of operation. These organizations are essentially prescriptive—senior people prescribe the answers (the thinking and the way to work) for more junior people to adopt. The so-called head office experts use their positions of power to tell the organization at large that employees should, for example, aim to be the best and practice core values such as integrity, respect, and a pioneering spirit. All the "telling" bumph emanating from head office is effectively propaganda aimed at brainwashing employees into the senior team's way of thinking and working (as if employees and middle managers did not think and work this way).

> "I'm telling you to agree to our core values of mutual respect, cooperation, and empowerment."

Where a contribution culture exists based on mutual respect and agreement, there is much less prescription. On behalf of the shareholders the chief executive will espouse the cause necessary to keep the company in business and growing. There will then be a series of agreements with team leaders throughout the company as to *what* each has to contribute in pursuit of the cause. Having agreed the contribution, each team leader and in turn each individual will have total freedom to find the best way to make that contribution.

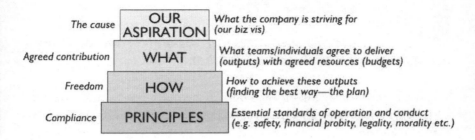

The above is a very simple model that provides maximum freedom and thus maximum motivation for every single employee and manager to contribute.

The following are some examples of agreed team contributions:

TEAM	CONTRIBUTION (RESULTS TO BE DELIVERED)
SALESPEOPLE	X sales revenue using Y budget
MARKETING	High % of market awareness using M budget
PRODUCTION	P output using Q budget
PERSONNEL	High morale, low employee turnover
FINANCE	Up-to-date and useful financial data
IT	Major systems improvements, effective control data company-wide
R&D	T new products developed and brought to market using R budget
ENGINEERING	D% downtime, E% efficiency using B budget
CUSTOMER RELATIONS	Very high % customer satisfaction using C budget

THE BIZ STEP 11

Ensure that each individual in your team has agreed the specific contribution that they are going to deliver.

BIZ POINT

People are employed to make a contribution through their work. It is critical that they are clear what that contribution is.

12 MEASURE WHAT IS IMPORTANT

Clarify and simplify the performance lines (measures) for each team member.

Spend a minute today asking each person in your team to state the five key performance lines by which their contribution is measured. Should there be any ambiguity, confusion, or misunderstanding, it is critical that you, as team leader, work with each team member to clarify, simplify, and agree their performance measures.

The best measures have three criteria. They are simple, they are important, and they are few in number. They are simple to understand and relatively simple to obtain data about. They are important because the business will be put at risk should the measurable line be crossed in the wrong direction. Finally, there should be few of them because most people are unable to recall more than four or five measures against which they judge their own performance.

The measures should be expressed through simple lines as follows:

RATING LINE	THIS IS MEASURE 1 OUT OF 5
105%	This is GREAT for the biz
100%	This is VERY GOOD for the biz
95%	This is GOOD for the biz
90%	This is the NORM for the biz
85%	This is BAD for the biz
80%	This is UNACCEPTABLE for the biz
75%	This is DANGEROUS for the biz

Too many companies have too many measures. They become obsessed with measurement and falsely believe that what cannot be measured cannot be done effectively. As a result, measures become meaningless and teams are burdened with useless bureaucracy.

The key factors that define any one person's contribution should be quantified (or qualified) in terms of four or five simple measurement lines for gauging their performance on a periodic basis. When these lines are clear motivation is high, because team members know exactly how their contribution will be assessed. Furthermore, they know that if their performance falls toward the line of unacceptability and the danger zone, action will be taken—unless they take action first. The following are five examples of deliverables.

ACCEPTABLE	Within budget (cost)	Above plan (revenue or output)	High quality (output)	Customer satisfaction	High morale
UNACCEPTABLE	Outside budget	Below plan	Low quality	Customer dissatisfaction	Low morale

For instance, in relation to the measure of morale, Henry Stewart of Happy Computers in London regularly carries out "happiness checks." What is important to him is that his company's customers and employees are happy. So he measures happiness and his aim is that no one should cross the line into unhappiness at work.

These simple measures form the essential discipline in the organization. Every employee will be able to understand them and will have at least one simple measurement line by which to gauge their own performance. These measures form the boundary lines around which an individual or a team's contribution is defined. In the absence of such a measure, performance will be poor and the business will suffer.

So measures are highly motivational. They enable people to know exactly what they are at work for and how they will be judged.

THE BIZ STEP 12
Work with your team to simplify measurement lines for each individual.

BIZ POINT
Keep your measures simple, meaningful, and few in number.

12

THE MAGIC SEVEN

When teams do the biz it's magic. It can take your breath away, it can be unbelievable—but it does actually happen. In the way these teams do things they are different from the mainstream of conventional business. There is a lack of convention and conformity and a high degree of originality and imagination. It excites customers, and employees are excited to work for these companies.

Some of the magic companies around today include eguk, the Virgin Group, Pret A Manger, Singapore Airlines, Happy Computers, Innocent Drinks, and Semco-Brazil.

The magic comes down to many of the little things that their people do on a day-by-day basis. These make a big difference to customers and as a result have a big impact on the business.

DISAPPEAR

Ensure that periodically you free yourself up from the workplace.

We have already noted that the best team leaders give top priority to their people and finding time for them. They are there when their people need them. But this does not mean that they have to be physically present all the time. If they are to allow their teams full freedom, one little thing they can do from time to time is to go away. When the boss disappears for a few hours or a few days the effect can be magical!

If you need to be permanently present, you are not doing your job properly. You are really showing people that you don't trust them, that you aren't prepared to train them to do your job.

Too many bosses demotivate their people by being there all the time, interfering and getting in the way of an effective operation. When they are around they think they have to do something and often do things that are unnecessary (such as ask for useless information).

Small

Regular

Large

BOSSES TO GO!

The pleasure—and privilege—in being a boss is to exercise the freedom of getting away and leaving the team to get on with it, knowing that they will do an excellent job in your absence. Most people heave a sigh of relief when the boss is not there. They feel freer and more relaxed knowing that there is no one breathing down their neck and no one being too inquisitive about what is going on.

If you are absent you are not in the best position to make decisions. This is all to the good, because it forces your team to make decisions on your behalf. The learning curve is very steep as a result. When you are present there is always a natural tendency for your people to refer decisions to you, just out of respect and also to prevent their own heads being blown off.

So to motivate your team you should find every excuse to absent yourself. This is where your creativity and imagination come in—there

32

are hundreds of little opportunities you can seize if you really want to get away and give your team a chance to show what they are made of. The following are some examples:

Disappear by:
- ✔ Putting yourself on a top-rate training program.
- ✔ Paying a visit to the outer reaches of the empire.
- ✔ Taking a secondment to internal audit.
- ✔ Going for a very long walk.
- ✔ Sitting on outside bodies (but not in the park or on the beach!).
- ✔ Doing charity work.
- ✔ Mystery shopping all your competitors.
- ✔ Taking a sabbatical to study "methods of iconic motivation."

The trick is…

Another trick is to run training programs and teach other people what you have failed to teach your team. There are always valuable lessons here—especially in being open and honest about your own shortcomings.

When you go away it is essential that you ask your team not to call you except in a dire emergency. You will defeat the whole object of the exercise if your mobile vibrates every five minutes with team members consulting you on the minor problems of everyday operations. Nor should it be necessary when you are away to check your email. Going away means being out of earshot, email reach, and eyesight.

THE BIZ STEP 13
Get out of the way by going away. Plan it now. Do it next week—or even tomorrow.

BIZ POINT
A team cannot remain permanently motivated when the boss is permanently around.

14 TELL STORIES

We all learn from stories. Become a storyteller and listen to other people's stories too.

There is nothing more magical than a good story. It lifts people's spirits and provides the essential lessons of life. Before words were written down the human race made immense progress by virtue of the stories told by village elders, shamans, and tribal chiefs. Those with the best stories were considered the wisest of all. Essentially it is through stories that we learn, not through textbooks and memorizing boring theories and data. The story amplifies the lesson with illustration and application.

The best team leaders love stories, knowing that they are vital for motivating the team. They take a genuine interest in the tales their people tell them and furthermore have some fascinating anecdotes to relate themselves.

At their best stories are fresh and record titbits of news from the previous day or two. Often there is a lesson that can be gleaned from the tale, for example about how a certain incident should or should not be handled, or how to talk with a certain individual, or what to avoid and what to take advantage of. These lessons are rarely written down but effectively create a body of experience that forms the basis of future decision making. The outcomes from all these stories will provide important lessons about the culture of the organization and how to behave in the future.

Stories also provide a stimulating diversion from the inevitable chores of everyday routine. If you eavesdrop on conversations you will invariably hear people telling each other stories about what happened earlier that day or the day before. When people go home they swap their stories of the day. Human beings are social animals and at the core of this socialization process is the exchange of stories. The best storytellers know how to excite people's interest with nuggets of news that are of immense appeal.

This is the story of what happened:

❖ When Nigel learnt he had been passed over for promotion again.
❖ When the chauffeur took the chairman to the wrong address.
❖ When the new computer broke down for the tenth time.
❖ When Vincent disagreed with the financial director.
❖ When Susie slipped on the wet floor in the toilet.
❖ On Janine's very first day with the company.
❖ When the CEO tried to serve a customer.
❖ When Abigail handed in her resignation.
❖ When Eduardo asked for a pay rise.

The way to become a good storyteller is to observe people's eyes as you tell them a story. You can easily detect whether or not they are interested, whether they are disengaging from your tale or enthralled by it. Equally, you can learn from your own response when listening to the stories of others. By analyzing how you feel you can discover the types of stories that attract you as opposed to turning you off. The lessons can then be applied to your own stories.

Emotional tone, passion, sensitivity, succinctness, a good finish and ending, together with intermittent "hook points" that sustain interest are all critical to the success of a story and the way it is told. Telling stories is a two-way process that depends on an interchange of motivational signals between transmitter (storyteller) and recipients (audience).

Storytelling does of course take time—and time has to be found if this essential motivational and learning process is to take place. The worst bosses never have time for stories and even punish people who tell them—for wasting time.

THE BIZ STEP 14

Start all team meetings with stories. Start each day with a story. The story doesn't have to be about work but should be about what's important to people (for example family, sport, vacations, weather, traffic, etc.).

BIZ POINT

Every team member has a story to tell. To motivate them, allow to tell their story and make sure that you listen carefully.

CELEBRATE ANY SUCCESS

To do the biz you need a culture of success and celebration. You can start today by celebrating yesterday's success.

When he was executive director of Starbucks Singapore, Michael Lee would say that his informal job title was director of celebrations. He saw one of his key tasks as visiting the 30 or so stores in Singapore and seizing every opportunity to discover successes that could be celebrated. It could be that a customer had written a complimentary letter, or a store had sold more muffins this week than last, or one of their part-time partners (as employees are called in Starbucks) had passed an important examination. They would celebrate all of these occasions. And at the regular conferences for store managers, Michael Lee would seek to identify successes in each store to be celebrated.

Contrast this with the experience of one salesperson in a major department store chain, who told me that after a couple of years working in the stationery department he was moved to carpets and floorings. Four weeks after joining his new department he succeeded in selling carpeting to the value of £10,000. He said to himself: "I've done it! I've managed at last to make a big-ticket sale!" He was thrilled with himself and went home and told his family. Sadly, at work not a single person recognized his achievement, let alone celebrated it.

> **"How dare you be successful? That's my job!"**

It is no wonder that many employees become dispirited because they see themselves as working hard and achieving a great deal without their magnificent results ever being celebrated. "My boss is on a performance-related incentive," one employee told me, "yet we front-liners are on a flat salary. Why should we work so hard only for the boss to benefit with a huge bonus as a result? He gets all the benefit and we don't benefit at all!"

Celebrating successes becomes a self-fulfilling prophecy. The more you look for successes to celebrate the more successes you will find—and thus the more success you will have. In doing so you focus people's minds on success and what it means to them. Conversely, the more you look for problems the more you will find them—and thus encounter problems wherever you turn.

Ken Lockett, an area manager with a major bank, tells a story of how he took over a team of branch managers. At their first team meeting he allowed them to set the agenda. All they did was state problems—for example, "We had a problem with our computers last week," "We had a problem with staff absenteeism," etc. He listened carefully and then at the end of the team meeting asked, "What successes did you have last week?" No one responded. "At our next team meeting I want you to tell me about your successes," Ken suggested. At first they struggled, but as the weeks passed they began to identify more successes. As an overall result the area jumped up the league of the bank's performance ratings. One of the little things Ken did was visit the branches in his area carrying a box of "celebration chocolates." He would approach managers and front-liners asking them, "What successes have you had over the last few days?" If they provided an answer (any success would do) he would offer them a chocolate.

Success is in the eye of the beholder. The key is therefore to make each success visible with a suitable declaration and celebration. It might be a simple celebratory card, or a bottle of champagne, or a box of chocolates, or a team lunch. The form of celebration does not matter— as long as there is a celebration. When your team scores at soccer you celebrate. You throw your arms up in the air and shout "Yes!" (or something to that effect). That's celebrating.

THE BIZ STEP 15

Go looking for at least one success a team member has enjoyed over the last week. Then crack open a bottle of champagne that you have personally purchased and celebrate with the team.

BIZ POINT
When there is nothing to celebrate life is pretty miserable.

15

TOUCH YOUR TEAM

Motivating a team touches their hearts with a little magic.

When it comes to touching team members, there are safe zones and danger zones. One danger zone is the heart, but it needs to be

touched. The safe zones are the hand, the elbow, the shoulder, and the eyes. All other parts of the body are banned.

To get to the danger zone of the heart you need to go through a safe zone first. That means reaching out to another person with inoffensive little behaviors that create an emotional connection.

These touching connections are an essential key to motivation and can be magical.

Here are some nice physical touches:

✔ Shake hands with team members whenever possible.
✔ Clasp the other person's elbow when shaking hands.
✔ Tap a person's shoulder when he or she has done something well.
✔ When walking and talking, guide the other person by the elbow.
✔ Pick a piece of fluff (or a hair) off a person's jacket and flick it away.
✔ If there is some sudden bad news, give an employee a sympathetic hug.
✔ Connect with the eyes and touch a person with the way you look at him or her.
✔ When an employee informs you of a personal problem, take his or her hand and pat it.

One team I knew developed the habit of slapping each other's hands every time they met.

The touch can be physical but does not have to be. For example, annotating a newspaper article that might interest a particular employee and leaving her a copy can be nice little touch. Taking a genuine interest, offering to help in some small way, sharing a confidence, or just opening the door for someone are all good little touches.

Your intention in touching another person must always be positive, with the aim of motivating them by presenting them with a token gift (the little touch) from your heart. The overall objective is to strike a connection that enhances the relationship, builds the team, and sparks sufficient emotional energy that people want to work for the boss concerned.

The best team leaders seem to be able to do this naturally. They take delight in reaching out to people and touching them in little ways that genuinely make them feel good. They know how to work a room and inject warm emotion into the maximum number of personal connections. These bosses create a great rapport as a result.

Even if touching does not come naturally it can be developed by practice, with the eventual result that it does in fact become natural. People can change if they want to. A cold, impersonal team leader can become a warm boss who personalizes relationships with such small touches.

The key is to keep the touch fresh and spontaneous rather than predictable and routine. As soon as touches appear artificial they lose their impact. They must be meant and that means that they must come from the heart.

THE BIZ STEP 16
Get in touch with what your people feel. Let them touch you with their thoughts and feelings and then demonstrate that you have been touched by what they say.

BIZ POINT
Learning about motivation involves discovering the positive touch points in people's lives.

16

17 CLEAN TOILETS, PUSH TROLLEYS, AND SERVE CUSTOMERS

From time to time, do the biz the way your team does it.

There is a consistent pattern among companies that deliver incredible results. From time to time the most senior executives like to be "hands on," to get out and about and do the biz themselves. They join in the spirit of things. When their people are under pressure and resources are short, they will clean toilets, push trolleys, sweep floors, load pallets, and serve customers.

John Black, who founded the restaurant chain Puccino's, will clean toilets when visiting one of his restaurants, just to help his team.

Richard Killoran, when he was general manager of Austin Reed's flagship clothing store in Regent Street, London, would devote every Saturday to serving customers. He would wander around and when he observed a "hot spot" (his staff being busy with customers) he would lend a helping hand and serve customers himself. He reckoned that he could perform 90 percent of the operations on the shopfloor.

The same principle applies in Pret A Manger, a renowned and rapidly expanding UK sandwich company. Everyone including the managing director has to undertake a regular stint in one of the stores, perhaps making sandwiches, serving customers, or stacking shelves.

To do the biz senior managers have to know what they are talking about and that means getting their hands dirty from time to time. Why expect your front-line people to deal effectively with an abusive customer when you have never dealt with one yourself? Too many managers spend too much time in high-rise ivory towers, pontificating at meetings, pumping out emails, and processing paper. As a result, they lose touch with reality. Reality is the operational interface between front-line employees and customers. It cannot be understood at second hand by reading reports. Reality has to be experienced if you are to keep in touch with it.

Richard Branson used to be renowned for pushing trolleys up and down the aisles when traveling on one of his Virgin flights. He would even amuse customers with magic tricks, but more importantly serving customers enabled him to listen carefully to what they had to say. It is far better to obtain feedback directly from customers than to study customer satisfaction statistics and scan through mystery shopping surveys.

When the boss gets involved and lends a helping hand, the spirit in a team changes. Team members become closer to those who manage them. They know that their bosses understand what is going on because they are there helping out.

Getting your hands dirty is motivational for everyone. For bosses it means using different muscles, thinking different thoughts, and getting away from the same old boring administrative routines. It gives them an opportunity to achieve something tangible, like pleasing customers directly, or improving the environment by tidying up, or enhancing a display by stacking shelves. It is fun too—and if they demonstrate that it is fun then in all probability their employees will find it fun in their turn.

THE BIZ STEP 17

Join in the spirit of things. Spend at least five minutes at the front line today and get your hands dirty. Stop talking. Do something revolutionary. If you haven't served a customer in the last ten years, serve one now. Experience how it feels. If you haven't cleaned a toilet in the last ten years, clean one now. Do it. Pick up litter, tidy shelves, answer phones, respond to complaints—aim to do the lot, but start with one activity today.

BIZ POINT
Managers have to know what they are talking about and that means getting their hands dirty from time to time.

17

18 INSPIRE TEAM MEMBERS

Stimulate the spirit in your people and inspire them.

You don't have to be Winston Churchill or Martin Luther King Jr. to inspire your people. You just have to be yourself. This means igniting the essential spirit that illuminates your unique soul and allowing it to energize those around you. You can inject a little of your spirit into your team members every day.

Most people like to be inspired, but not all bosses are inspirational. While it is essential to motivation, inspiration is not something that can be produced by following a procedure or implementing a personnel policy. Inspiration is a spark or trigger and it is magical in its effect. It comes when we hear a story that touches our heart. It comes when someone says something that strikes a chord with us. It comes when our breath is taken away by some outstanding performance. It can galvanize us into taking action ourselves to do even better.

Inspiration is like an emotional lightning conductor that flashes through to an individual's soul. It is not a logical thought process and no manner of reasoning can spark it.

Inspiration is difficult to define although it is easy to sense. We feel inspired when new horizons open before us and we sense we can reach out beyond the entrenched limits we have set for ourselves.

Those who inspire us awaken a desire in us to do even better. They help us realize our potential to go even further than we think we can.

The best bosses sense when their people are low, tired and jaded, miserable and defeatist, full of pain from working too hard for too long and for too little. They breathe fresh spirit into their teams, awakening their senses, restoring their beliefs, and recharging their batteries. This is inspirational. It is a new energy and it comes from the little things these bosses do.

"Inspiration" is all to do with "spirit" and putting spirit "in" to people. When people talk of team spirit, they are describing an indefinable essence that sets a group of people apart from others who are just going through the motions.

The inspiration to get people out of a rut or to achieve the most difficult goals does not have to come from a rousing speech full of eloquent rhetoric. In fact it can come from little touches that act as a spark to reignite a passion. It might be a knowing wink, a warming smile, a brief word of acknowledgment, a kind word of understanding, or even a precious five minutes with a boss. It might come when a boss takes an interest in a

INSPIRATION

Spirit   Magic   Spark   Stimulus

Encouragement   Passion   Imagination

Delight   Enlightenment   Excitement

Enthusiasm   Exhilaration   Energy

MOTIVATION

problem and helps an individual find a way through. Or it might occur when someone finds well-chosen words of encouragement.

When we are inspired we are lifted onto a high. It can never last, but even so it is sufficient to carry us forward for a short period. In due course we will need further inspiration. There are a variety of sources. Some people go to religious texts for inspiration, while others seek it from current icons and the heroes of the past. Others find it in their mentors, coaches, and counselors.

Ideally team leaders should provide the inspiration for a magnificent contribution at work. When managers succeed in this they transform themselves from people administering the mundane routines of everyday work to inspirational leaders who are taking their people forward.

THE BIZ STEP 18

Ask your team what inspires them, then go and find that inspiration for them.

Furthermore, seek inspiration yourself from your team. If you think they are great this should inspire you.

BIZ POINT

Inspire, aspire, respire, perspire, inspire...

18

19 WRITE, RING, AND REMEMBER

Write team members little notes, ring them when they least expect it, and remember their anniversaries.

The main theme of this book is that it is the little things that make a big difference to team leadership and motivation. The advantage of little things is that they can be personal and are not a product of an impersonal, centralized personnel policy. No such policy can legislate for all the small but exceptionally important things team leaders can do. For example, you can't have a policy that states: "Say positive things about Jackie's new hairstyle." Personalization is a key motivational driver. It requires you to seize some of the infinite number of opportunities every day to motivate people. A

Christmas card that is personalized with an apt little comment such as "glad to hear that Don is out of hospital and will be back home to enjoy Christmas with you" is far more effective than a simple signature or a printed statement without specific reference to the recipient.

Tim Waterstone, when he used to head up a chain of bookstores, said, "Every day I try to write at least six notes to members of staff. If I see a display in a Waterstones window that is particularly good, then I will drop a note to say so."

These little things are so easy to do and it is a wonder that most bosses neglect them. Here are some examples:

SEND AN IMPROMPTU EMAIL OR TEXT MESSAGE

❖ "Harold, just to let you know that I bumped into Kathryn yesterday and she asked after you."
❖ "Martha, best of luck with the Oslo project. I am sure you will do a great job."
❖ "I've just come out of a meeting with our CEO, who said your report was extremely helpful."
❖ "Thanks for staying late last evening, Evelyn, it was much appreciated."

WRITE NOTES

❖ Drop a note to say how pleased you were with Betty's presentation.

❖ Send a card in the internal post to thank Roland for all his help in sorting out the transportation problem.

❖ Leave a sticky note on Hamid's computer screen to say that you like his new screensaver.

❖ Attach a personalized note to an article that will interest Tracy.

RING PEOPLE WHEN THEY LEAST EXPECT IT

❖ When on an overseas trip, spend half an hour calling various team members, not to discuss work but just to find out how they are.

❖ Call Tom's wife at home one evening to thank her for putting up with all the long hours he has been working to complete the project.

❖ Call George to ask him whether he saw the match last night and what he thought of the goal.

❖ Give Mary a call to ask how her mother is as you've just learnt that she's gone into a home.

REMEMBER ANNIVERSARIES

❖ Ensure that every team member receives a birthday card with an appropriate comment.

❖ On the anniversary of a team member joining the company, send them a little card to thank them for their support over the last year.

❖ Invent eccentric if not unusual anniversaries and send cards, for example to celebrate the anniversary of the day William made his first five-figure sale (you'll need to keep a diary for this purpose).

❖ Discover when team members are celebrating major anniversaries (such as ten years of marriage) and send a special card to their home.

There are thousands of different and creative ways you can use emails, text messages, notes, phone calls, or cards to motivate people.

THE BIZ STEP 19

Discipline yourself to send one unexpected message and make one unexpected call to a team member every day. Every week hunt down anniversaries to celebrate with an appropriate card.

BIZ POINT
Never make writing notes, making calls, and celebrating anniversaries a routine. Each should be spontaneous, original, and unexpected.

SEVEN BIZ PERFORMERS

Doing the biz is all about performance and delivering what customers expect, what shareholders want, and what the team needs.

There are a number of performance-enhancing behaviors that a team leader can adopt to motivate the team further. These are little things that will have a big impact on the way team members go about their work.

Seven biz performers are selected for this part of the book:

20 TAKE THE LEAD IN BECOMING THE BEST

Unless you attempt to take the lead you cannot be a leader.

Being a leader is about taking the lead and about all the little things you do to achieve this. For example, it might be about taking the lead in providing a new buzzing style of service to customers and all the little steps necessary to create this buzz (see *The Buzz*, the companion book to this one). It might be about taking the lead in getting intractable problems sorted out, for example volunteering at your management meeting to get the car parking problem fixed.

There is a great deal of debate about the difference between a manager and a leader. The answer is simple. A leader is a person who aims to be the best in a designated arena and takes the initiative in becoming so. Becoming a leader is not a right that is assigned to an employee by virtue of promotion to supervision or management. A real leader is someone who wants to take the lead, who wants to pick up the ball, run with it, score goals, and put their team in a winning position. Effective leaders don't wait to be told what to do. They do it first because they are the first to see the need and seize the opportunity. Whatever the size of their team and whatever their place in the organization, leaders are a driving force in doing the biz. At one level it might mean taking the lead in resolving a complex customer complaint, at another taking the lead in raising quality standards. A leader is a person who owns and resolves a problem, who detects a need for change and then takes responsibility for effecting it. A leader seizes accountability.

Taking the lead means seeking out opportunities for improvement and following them, whether they are new ways to please customers or even better ways of motivating the team.

Here are some examples of the kind of lead you can take as a team leader in order to be the best:

48

- ✔ Work exceptionally hard to achieve the best results for the business so that you never let the company down and are always in the lead when it comes to meeting if not exceeding targets.
- ✔ Pioneer new ways of motivating your team so that you become a leading example in the company of generating high morale (for example, agreeing that they can work at home whenever they think best).
- ✔ Take the lead in encouraging your team to win awards, prizes, and any other accolades that reflect their excellence.
- ✔ Do your best to fight battles on behalf of your team when you genuinely feel they deserve better (for example, obtaining the latest and most up-to-date training).

- ✔ Pushing back the boundaries of service to your customers (internal or external) by aiming to be world-class in everything you and the team do for them.
- ✔ Become the spokesperson for all that is best in the company, speaking at conferences, writing articles, and generally extolling the virtues of working there (and thus becoming one of its customers).
- ✔ Achieve the highest standards by leading the way in getting all the little things right, paying attention to detail, and ensuring that these little things make a big difference.
- ✔ Take the lead in ensuring that your team has the best and latest equipment, whether it relates to computing, telecommunications, or any other system.

Invariably, leadership is about winning and creating an organization where the team wins, the customer wins, and overall the company wins.

THE BIZ STEP 20
Sit back with your team and reflect on what the best means to your biz, and then take the lead in achieving this.

BIZ POINT
Taking the lead to be the best requires you to aspire to be the best.

20

21 CREATE PERFORMANCE LINES IN YOUR MIND

A team leader should take action if anyone transgresses lines of acceptable performance, behavior, and discipline.

There is no such thing as a straight line in the natural world. Any study of growing things will reveal lots of curves and jagged edges, but no straight lines. You can peer at trees, leaves, flowers, bodies, hair, skin, and any other natural substance, but you will never detect a straight line. Even a drawn straight line is not perfectly straight but an approximation of straightness.

The best place for straight lines is in people's minds, determining the boundaries in their lives that should not be crossed. This is essential for a boss doing the biz. Before you can motivate people they need to be perfectly clear about the lines of performance, behavior, and discipline that they should keep on the right side of and never transgress. Without such lines there is a high risk of disorganization, disorder, and exceptionally poor performance.

This can be demonstrated in the following diagram:

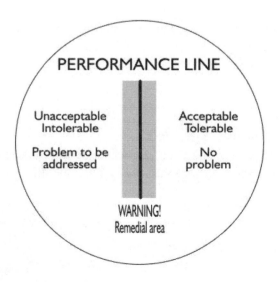

PERFORMANCE LINE

Unacceptable
Intolerable

Problem to be
addressed

Acceptable
Tolerable

No
problem

WARNING!
Remedial area

When the performance or behavior of any team member declines toward the warning or remedial area, immediate action must be taken by the team leader. Failure to do so will lead to poor team performance. The action required is normally a warning.

If the team member is unable to improve performance and cross back to the right side of the line, it is essential that this person is told to leave the team. No boss can live with circumstances that are unacceptable and intolerable in contributing to the future success of the team and the company.

Examples of what constitutes the line differentiating the acceptable from the unacceptable are provided in Chapter 12 on measurement. It is imperative for any team leader to develop very strong and clearly defined lines in their own mind about acceptable and unacceptable performance and behavior. A boss's credibility will suffer immeasurably if he or she declares such a line and then allows it to be transgressed without taking action. In this case these declarations become idle threats and people will be seen to be "getting away with murder."

Bosses who have fuzzy lines or no lines of performance, behavior, and discipline in their minds readily lose respect and are difficult to deal with. You don't know where you stand with them because you don't know where they draw the line.

THE BIZ STEP 21
Test yourself by writing down one performance line that you have in your mind that no team member should cross.

BIZ POINT
A boss without boundaries is bound to fail.

22 PUT YOURSELF ON THE LINE

To do the biz you need to be 100 percent clear about your own line of accountability.

On rare occasions there is one particular thing you need to do that will have a big impact on the biz and your future: to put your job on the line.

You can't do this unless you are clear about what the line is. It is the line of accountability, which is the most important line for any team leader who wants to motivate a team to do the biz.

Accountability means being held to account for literally everything that happens within the boundaries of your designated area of responsibility.

THE LINE OF THE DISCIPLINED MIND

Accountable | Not accountable

When lines of accountability are fuzzy or non-existent, it is difficult to manage effectively and there will be a tendency toward bureaucracy and inefficiency as the buck is passed around until someone can own up to making a decision.

When the lines of accountability are clear there is no room for excuses. Either you are accountable or not. In too many organizations lack of clarity in accountability leads to what is called the "blame syndrome," scapegoating, or witchhunts as other departments are blamed for shortcomings and failings in overall performance. Nobody owns up to anything that goes wrong. It also leads to passing the buck. No one will make a decision.

One example of fuzzy accountability is when head office functions hire people and then impose the new recruit on line departments with vacancies. When lines of accountability are clear managers take complete responsibility for selecting new team members, knowing that they will be held accountable for managing the performance of that person. You cannot have other people deciding who should or should not be in your team.

The same relates to training. You as team leader are accountable for training your team and cannot blame head office for failing to deliver that training. By hook or by crook you have to make sure that it happens. That is accountability. It is being accountable for choosing all the inputs (resources) necessary to deliver the outputs (production and sales) and the desired results.

In companies where accountabilities are clear, managers agree the contribution to be made, the principles or standards to be complied with, along with the necessary budget—and get on and deliver accordingly. There is no argument about this.

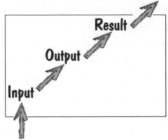

TOTAL ACCOUNTABILITY

Too often managers agree objectives and then find that they are unable to deliver on them because of head office restrictions, for example relating to travel or expenditure on new equipment. If this threatens output delivery then team leaders who aim to do the biz will put their jobs on the line and fight for the resources and freedoms that they believe necessary to make the contribution to which they have committed.

Bosses who fight their corner in this way will be highly respected by their teams. They will be great motivators because the teams will know that they will do everything possible to help the team members deliver what they want in order to do the biz.

THE BIZ STEP 22
Reflect on this chapter and identify in what circumstances you would put your job on the line. What is that line?

BIZ POINT
The best team leaders are those who have sufficient courage to put their jobs on the line if necessary.

22

23 WORK HARD

Success is a function of hard work. The harder you work, the greater your contribution will be.

Unless you feel tired at the end of the working day you have not been working effectively. When you feel tired is the time to stop—but that does not mean that feeling tired is bad or wrong. The trap is to take it easy and avoid the difficult stuff that saps energy.

Any success in life—whether completing a marathon, winning a competition, or even writing a book—requires hard work. It means applying concentrated doses of energy to accomplish each intermediate step of the plan as well as to cope with the unplanned.

Team leaders who do the biz have learnt that lesson and developed a hard-working style. They are so committed and passionate about what they do that they are prepared to put a considerable amount of effort hour by hour and day by day into achieving the desired results. They know that the harder they personally work and the harder the team works, the greater the probability of success in relation to the competition.

When in hard work mode they resist any amusing diversions and distractions in order to focus their energies on the desired end result that day, whether it means speaking to 50 customers, meeting 50 employees, or making 50 telephone calls. On rare occasions this means putting in long hours, starting early, finishing late, and working through lunch. But not on every occasion, because that is dangerous. Working hard is not synonymous with long hours. Nor is it synonymous with being a workaholic who never stops. Doing the biz means putting focused effort into the time you are on the job.

It is easy to motivate people to work hard. They just have to have a good reason for doing so—and the boss's task is to ensure that this reason (the cause) is effectively communicated, is understood, and is subscribed to with a high degree of passion and commitment.

Furthermore, people need to enjoy what they are doing. Team members are more likely to work hard when they are having fun doing so and can see some tangible results from their efforts.

Hard work is not merely about physical energy. It is also about adrenalin and emotional energy. These are essential ingredients to keep any individual or team going. The will to work hard emanates from the heart, not the mind. Logic will always step in and say "don't work as hard" and at times it is right to apply this logic. However, what powers people on and on and on is the adrenalin and the emotional drives asserting that this objective is so important to us that we must devote all our available energies to achieving it.

When it comes to improvement, doing the biz means practice and practice and practice. That is hard work—but it is what the superstars do. Opera singer Pavarotti once said, "I practice one hundred times to be good while others only practice ten times." Golfer Tiger Woods commented, "The harder I practice the luckier I become." The more you work hard at practicing and improving what you do, the greater success you will have.

Hard work involves sacrifice. It means going without the easier and more pleasurable things while concentrating your energies on attaining the desired result. The pleasure can come later when you stop work.

THE BIZ STEP 23
Discuss with your team what hard work means in practice. Encourage them to define it and apply it.

BIZ POINT
The harder the competition, the harder the work to be done.

24 PRAISE REGULARLY AND REPRIMAND RARELY

Focus on praising people and helping them find better ways when things go wrong.

Shoshila tells a story about her manager, Ravi, when a customer complained about a lack of response from the hotel in Mauritius where they worked. The customer had sent a fax from Paris seeking confirmation of a reservation. Shoshila was about to end her shift and found the computer system freezing up on her. So she left the fax to be dealt with by a colleague about to come on shift. Five days later there was a second fax from the customer stating: "Given your failure to respond to my previous fax I have made a reservation elsewhere and no longer require the one I thought I had made with your hotel."

When Ravi saw this he simply drew an unhappy face on the customer's fax, signed the drawing, and passed it back to Shoshila (along with a copy of his response to the customer).

"We knew we had made a major mistake and lost vital business and customer goodwill during difficult times," explained Shoshila, "but Ravi did not say a word. He just drew this miserable face and passed it back to us. We knew we had let him down and had upset him."

It was a rare reprimand and one given with the lightest of touches. When people make mistakes there is no need to bear heavily down on them as some bosses do with their storming, shouting, witchhunts, and severe warnings. These bosses create a culture of intimidation and fear in which mistakes are never made for the simple reason that front-line people never make decisions—they leave them to the bosses.

Too much reprimanding leads to defenses being erected and failure not being admitted. People become hard because they see their bosses as hard. This is counter-productive.

Managers who do the biz prefer to focus on praising people, while still accepting that they occasionally make mistakes. The time to reprimand someone is not when a mistake has been made, but when they don't learn any lessons from that mistake.

> "If there is one thing I can praise my team leader for, it's that she is always praising me."

Lyn Graham is chief internal auditor at Portsmouth City Council in the UK. When a mistake is made she always asks her team, "What did I do wrong?" She never blames the team or its individual members. Instead, she looks at herself and asks, "What could I have done better to avoid the team making this mistake?"

One of the key tasks of a team leader is to seek out examples of excellent performance and then praise team members for it. Most people welcome praise provided that it is sincere, genuine, and reflects some significant aspect of their work. Nobody likes false praise or bosses who use superficial praise as a cheap motivational device.

Nevertheless, it is not difficult to seek out opportunities to give genuine praise and this is what the best team leaders do. In addition to seeking out good performance, they also identify the characteristics they like about people and praise them for these.

A kind word of praise for the good things someone has done is far better than continually reprimanding them for the things they have not done. (There is more on how to give praise in *The Buzz*, the companion book to this one.)

THE BIZ STEP 24

Find five genuine things to praise about your team today—and then go and praise them. Meanwhile, forget about reprimanding people.

BIZ POINT
There is nothing like genuine praise to boost an individual's self-esteem.

24

25 BE STRAIGHT

Let team members know where they stand with you.

Everything little thing you do as a boss will be observed by your team and used as evidence in forming their opinion of you. When you are not straight with people, second-guessing becomes the order of the day. By being straight with team members you encourage them to be straight with you.

Lack of straightness in communication happens all the time. People are always having to interpret each other's behavior, for the simple reason that few feel able to be totally honest with others. In suppressing our thoughts and feelings about team members we inadvertently allow our behavior to do the talking for us. It is the look on our face rather than the words we utter, it is the action we take rather the words that explain it. It is when a friend passes us by and does not even say hello. It

Straight talk needed

is when a colleague criticizes us behind our back. It is when our boss neglects to invite us to an important meeting.

One reason team leaders are not straight is because they don't want to demotivate people. They are afraid that people would rather not hear what they have to say, or that open and honest criticism will damage a team member's self-esteem and the individual will react defensively. Therefore they avoid the risk of spelling things out.

The whole area of being open and honest with people is thus fraught with difficulty. That is why so many bosses turn a blind eye, tolerate perceived poor performance, and only take action when it is too late. Too often people are fired for doing a bad job when all along they thought they were doing a good one. Nobody had been straight with them and informed them otherwise.

The solution to this conundrum lies in the purpose of being straight. If the intention is to hurt the person by making him or her look foolish, then obviously you should withhold the remark. Too many people speak their minds with the intention of putting another person down.

However, if the intention is to help the individual by drawing attention to some opportunity for improvement, being straight is essential.

The setting for the communication is also important. If you are going to be straight with a person it is best to do it one-to-one rather than in public. It is also best to give some prior thought to how you are going to handle the communication.

On balance, people respect team leaders who tell them where they stand. They need to have answers to the following basic questions:

❖ "Does my boss think I am doing a good job or not?"
❖ "Does my boss let me know when he feels good about me?"
❖ "Does my boss let me know when she feels bad about me?"
❖ "Does my boss want me to be successful?"
❖ "Does my boss really care about the contribution I make?"

People are motivated when they know what is inside the team leader's mind, what they are thinking and feeling, and how this affects them as team members. They respect bosses who are completely open and honest. There are no hidden corners of negative thinking, of bad feelings, of grudges and dislikes, let alone of favored and unfavored people. With these team leaders everything is out on the table. If one team member moves out of line the team leader steps in and is straight with him or her: "I am not happy with the way you reacted to your colleague."

Bosses who do the biz pick up and comment constructively on the little things, because they know that it is these that make a big difference.

THE BIZ STEP 25

Make a point of sitting down regularly with your people to tell them what you think of them. Encourage them to be straight with you too. You need to know what they think of you.

BIZ POINT
The team leaders whom people respect most
are those who are straight with them.

25

26 FIRE POOR PERFORMERS

Never tolerate persistent substandard performance. It is better to fire people than for customers to fire your company.

Nobody likes to fire people, but it has to be done. There will come a time in every manager's career when someone who has not performed needs to be let go. You cannot put everyone else at risk by tolerating persistent substandard performance, which risks not only the reputation of the business with customers but your commitment to shareholders. If a team member consistently fails to deliver the agreed contribution or comply with the accepted standards, then he or she has to leave.

In a highly competitive world there are always winners, runners-up, and people who come third. These people normally survive. However, coming last there will always be a small minority of misfits who never seem able to perform, no matter how much they promise

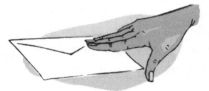

and no matter how much encouragement is given by a team leader. These people can be a huge drain on a boss's time and energies.

Jack Welch turned this process into a fine art, commanding his managers every year to identify the worst performers and fire them. His approach was stark and controversial, but General Electric's outstanding results during his 20 years there seem to bear out its success.

While it feels good to be nice to people, when necessary the team leader has to be prepared to call an underperforming individual into the office and say, "Enough is enough, the line has been crossed, you haven't delivered despite all the improvement opportunities, now is the time for you to go."

You can make the process for firing people as pleasant as possible, giving them generous checks and even saying some nice things for the record, but in the end you have to be tough to survive as a boss. You cannot allow a poor performer to drag the team down. As investment expert Jim Slater said many years ago, "One has to be ruthless in decision and compassionate in execution—when it comes to firing people."

Firing people can in fact be highly motivational, not only for the team members who remain but also for the victim. As one person said when asked to leave an organization, "I don't want to work for a company that fires me."

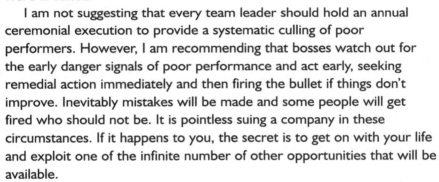

A lot of people bounce back after being sacked, invigorated after a merciful release from a job to which they could hardly admit to themselves they were ill-suited.

I am not suggesting that every team leader should hold an annual ceremonial execution to provide a systematic culling of poor performers. However, I am recommending that bosses watch out for the early danger signals of poor performance and act early, seeking remedial action immediately and then firing the bullet if things don't improve. Inevitably mistakes will be made and some people will get fired who should not be. It is pointless suing a company in these circumstances. If it happens to you, the secret is to get on with your life and exploit one of the infinite number of other opportunities that will be available.

It should be stressed that to be fair to everyone, a good boss will agree with the team what constitutes poor performance and where the line between that and good performance is drawn. Everyone should understand where that line is.

THE BIZ STEP 26
Focus today on the danger signals of poor performance. Can you recognize poor performance when you see it—and can you deal with it effectively?
If you don't put other people's jobs on the line for poor performance, your own job will be at risk.

BIZ POINT
Aim never to fire people. But when you do, be sure of your aim.

26

BIZ TEAMS

Invisible, intangible, indeterminate, indefinable—but essential. That's the spirit. With no team spirit there is no biz, just cold lifeless factories and endless corridors of vending machines.

Spirit is the essence of all motivation. It can't be purchased from a shelf nor injected into an individual. It emanates from the soul and is at the core of our unique self. It drives us forward and keeps us going. When the spirit dries up we stop.

The best team leaders show spirit in motivating their people, while the worst bosses put a lid on it for fear of unleashing the genie—the genius of people.

When you have spirit you have a team. When there is no spirit the team will fall apart.

27 DIGNIFY TEAM MEMBERS

Everyone wants to be treated with dignity. If others only recognized this the world would be a better place. Treat every single person you encounter today with the utmost dignity.

Putting people down is all too common. It is the malicious remark, the scowl, the throwaway gesture, the angry comment. And it is the constant criticism of others. It is always other people who don't know best, who could do better if only they thought and acted like us—because we know best.

Such an approach is pernicious. We are not even aware of it, but much of what we say about people attacks their dignity. In attempting to enhance our own dignity, with the trappings of executive power and prestige, we diminish that of others.

Conversely, the team leaders who are incredibly effective at motivating people are those who treat the members of their team with the utmost dignity. This is reflected in a multitude of small behaviors that enhance the self-esteem of team members.

The reason these bosses act this way is simple. It is because the best team leaders:

- ✔ Like people.
- ✔ Treat people with dignity.
- ✔ Are "of the people."
- ✔ Respect people for what they are.
- ✔ Help people through difficult times.
- ✔ Tolerate mistakes and learn from them.
- ✔ Do not make jokes at an employee's expense.
- ✔ Do not show people up when things go wrong.
- ✔ Do not go on witchhunts or seek out scapegoats.
- ✔ Do not judge people badly when their weaknesses show up.
- ✔ Do not make matters worse when something embarrassing happens.

Related closely to dignity is self-esteem and the sense of worth that any individual has. We all have incredibly sensitive antennae when it comes to assessing whether this person or that genuinely values us as individuals. When that value is shown, we enjoy a sense of dignity.

Dignifying team members requires a wide range of small, positive behaviors to be demonstrated. In addition to the ones stated above, here are some more of the little things good team leaders do. They:

✔ Listen carefully to what employees say and treat their opinions with great respect.
✔ Look for the good things that employees do (rather than the mistakes that they make).
✔ Express genuine appreciation for the contribution that people make.
✔ Are totally open and honest with team members.
✔ Are influenced by team members.
✔ Treat people as equals.
✔ Give time to people.
✔ Enjoy the company of team members.
✔ Reveal their hearts to team members, showing them their feelings (hopefully positive).
✔ Express through every little thing they do, including their body language, eyes, and words, that team members are very important to them.
✔ Demonstrate that they really trust employees (for example by taking them into their confidence).

Is this my boss?

THE BIZ STEP 27

With the help of a thesaurus, list as many words as you can that relate to dignity.

Then identify a behavior that relates to each word. Practice applying these behaviors and thus dignifying people.

BIZ POINT
Act with dignity in all your business dealings—
with your customers, suppliers, and team
members.

27

28 COOPERATE AND CREATE A "YES" SPIRIT

Work together with everyone to avoid them working against you. Say "yes" whenever possible.

Cooperation is another word for "yes." An alternative take on it is "rely on me for help."

One of the little things a team leader can do is to say "yes" to as many requests as possible. There is a broad cluster of other terms that reflect the same underlying spirit:

✔ Mutual support and mutual respect ("yes" to helping).
✔ Sharing and caring for each other ("yes" to consideration and compassion).
✔ Partnership ("yes" to working together).
✔ Collaboration ("yes" to a joint effort).
✔ Unity ("yes" to a common purpose).
✔ Teamwork ("yes" to putting the team before individuals).

Cooperation within and among teams is essential for doing the biz. In all organizations goals are shared and we need to work in a cooperative spirit to achieve them. No employee or manager can be so insular that they do their own thing all the time. The overall goals of the company are for the greater good and it thus requires a degree of personal sacrifice to achieve them. It means forgiving differences, bearing no grudges, and doing more for the company than we would for ourselves or our immediate team.

In the absence of cooperation we get the word "no." This often leads to battles and wars within the organization, more commonly described as internal politics. When this happens people play vicious games behind each other's backs and try to do down their "enemies" while seeking to impress the powers that be.

The person who suffers is often the customer. Vital information is not transmitted across departmental boundaries as employees close in defensively within their own battle lines. "It's not my problem" is the common cry when there is a lack of cooperation. Employees are reluctant to venture out and help other departments in need—they don't answer other people's telephones and don't want to deal with a customer's problem that takes them outside the confines of departmental routines.

Furthermore, initiatives from elsewhere are resisted as "not invented here," so that team members can focus solely on meeting their own parochial needs. In such companies, the motivated innocents who do help others become willing horses that get flogged. The more difficult and prickly staff, demotivated as they are, succeed in avoiding the action and are never seen to cooperate.

The first and most important step to countering this is a "yes" signal from a team leader that cooperation within the team and with other teams is mandatory.

The next step is to redefine the boundaries, pushing them well beyond the individual and the team to encompass the common good of the company as a whole. The more narrowly a job is defined, the less likely there is to be cooperation. The third step is to confront those difficult people who seem reluctant to cooperate, encouraging them to reverse their approach. Fourthly, you need to cross demarcation lines, consulting on and agreeing with others a simple code of conduct on how to work together. This need not be written down but should be well understood by virtue of the ethos practiced in the organisation. When most people are seen to be cooperating with each other, the message is clear and need not be stated.

Cooperation means putting yourself out and hesitating ten times before saying "no" to any request for help. It also means volunteering whenever possible. Cooperation can be hard work, because it involves working for outsiders as well as those inside your team.

THE BIZ STEP 28
Put cooperation on the agenda of your next meeting and explore what it means in practice in terms of saying "yes."

BIZ POINT
"Yes" is one of the most exciting words in the biz world.

28

IDENTIFY MOTIVATIONS

To motivate team members you need to understand what motivates them.

It is impossible to force people into a mold. It is their choice whether they want to shape up in the way you want. Cloning sheep is controversial enough and so cloning people should definitely be out. Yet many companies

Uniformity is the enemy of individuality

try to clone their employees, insisting they be what the company wants them to be as opposed to what they, as individuals, want to be. It is assumed that what motivates one person is what motivates another. Therefore motivation programs are intended for all but applicable to only a few.

The key for any team leader in motivating team members is to help them identify and achieve what they want to be

in life and at work. This requires no more than a little time sitting down with each team member and talking to them.

The following are some typical responses when people are asked what motivates them:

- ❖ "I want to make a difference in what I do at work."
- ❖ "I love to travel and this job provides me with the opportunity."
- ❖ "I'm a bit of a show-off really so that's why I demonstrate products to customers."
- ❖ "I just love pleasing customers."
- ❖ "I get a kick from solving problems. The bigger a customer's problem, the more I love it."
- ❖ "I look forward to coming to work because we have a great team and I love to be with them."
- ❖ "I like this job because I am always learning new things. I have developed enormously here."
- ❖ "I'll be honest. I need the money and I work here because the pay is good."
- ❖ "What motivates me is a fear of failure. I never let people down."
- ❖ "There is nothing like a challenge. It's great when my boss throws a challenge at me."
- ❖ "I just want to be liked and loved, to be honest with you. When I am praised and appreciated then I am motivated."
- ❖ "This is a great company. Everything is high quality here. It is important to me that I am associated with this type of business."
- ❖ "A sense of achievement is what motivates me. I am always wanting to achieve things."

In other words, we are all different when it comes to what motivates us. Not everyone is motivated to make a presentation, write reports, travel to distant parts of the world, or deal with stroppy customers. Some people are happy enough to do the same thing day in and day out, while others would hate that and require the stimulus of frequent change. Some people like office work and others hate it.

Understanding individual motivation means moving away from the traditional "tell" approach to one of listening, understanding, and encouraging. Traditional methods of motivation are hierarchical and predicated on a mindset of "I know best because I'm the boss and therefore you must do as I say." This is the old-fashioned command-and-control approach. It takes no account of variations in individual motivation.

As soon as a team leader has been able to identify the motivational drivers of any one individual, he or she is then in a position to help that person move in the desired direction. For example, if someone really wants to make a difference to the organization, the two can explore together what this really means in practice.

The process of identifying individual motivations means accepting people for what they are and want to be. It requires a demonstration of respect for the choices they have made in life and at work and the consequences these have brought.

Dan Paul, a store manager with ODEL, a retail chain in Sri Lanka, starts every day with a short motivation meeting with his team, to focus on what is going to motivate them today.

THE BIZ STEP 29
Spend five minutes with each of your team members and ask them a simple question: "What motivates you?"

BIZ POINT
By identifying motivations we help people bring out the best in themselves.

29

30 LET PEOPLE EXPRESS THEMSELVES

Create the time and the climate for people to express themselves freely and openly.

Freedom has two related dimensions: the freedom to make decisions and the freedom to express yourself.

Nobody is going to speak up if they fear their boss is going to slap them down in public, ridicule them, or consistently reject their ideas. When feelings and thoughts are suppressed it is dangerous for the organization. Bosses begin to lose touch with their people and fail to understand what is going on.

> **THE BIZ TEAM**
> Who sets
> the agenda
> for team meetings?

For a team to thrive and be motivated it is essential for its leader to create frequent opportunities for people to express freely whatever they want to say. Team members need to feel confident that they can take any issue to their boss, no matter how personal or how small and apparently inconsequential, and that the boss will listen carefully.

At team meetings the agenda needs to be sufficiently open that team members have the opportunity to speak their minds and be given a fair hearing.

This places great demands on a boss. If people are allowed to speak up, some will tend to criticize the team leader for the shortcomings in the business. Equally, there will be a natural tendency for the boss to become defensive and to reject such criticism as unfounded. These negative circuits of blame and defense must be avoided, which can only be done by encouraging people to express themselves in ways that lead to positive conclusions.

The best bosses agree informal codes of conduct when it comes to open debate. They agree that there will be no personal comment that attempts, deliberately or otherwise, to damage a person's esteem and reputation.

While it is important to let off steam, it is also important to channel the steam in a direction that powers the team forward.

The real skill is carefully listening with a view to obtaining an in-depth understanding of what team members think and feel. By providing frequent opportunity for this, issues can be identified early and addressed, as opposed to being left to fester. Thus it is far more important for Fred to discover at an early stage that Fran is unhappy with the job she is doing than to find this out six months later when she resigns. By encouraging Fran to express how she feels about her work, her team leader can do his best to address the factors that are making her unhappy.

Good team leaders discipline themselves not to react when something outrageous is said, but to probe carefully and get to the root cause of any problem. Not everyone is able to express themselves in a clear, succinct, and articulate way.

The organization will always suffer when people feel bad. To counter this, they must be given the earliest possible opportunity to express any bad feelings, thus maximizing the prospect of addressing the issues involved and remotivating the team.

One of the little things a boss can do to motivate a team is to create relaxed, informal sessions with open agendas when team members can express their thoughts and feelings collectively about what is going on. This should also be done on a one-to-one basis, allowing each individual to say whatever is on their mind. An open door is equally important so that people can bring issues to the boss when they arise.

THE BIZ STEP 30

From time to time sit down with your team in a relaxed environment and ask them a simple question: "Please tell me openly and honestly how you feel about what is going on at the moment." This should also be done individually in a series of one-to-one meetings.

BIZ POINT
Without expression there is little
understanding.

30

31 SHOW TEAM MEMBERS YOU CARE

Demonstrate care every day. It is a driving force for team leaders who do the biz.

A lot of time is wasted talking about core values. These don't need to be invented through academic debate or facilitated forums, because core to any business are a set of prima facie values that are so intrinsic that they are virtually indisputable. One such core value is "care."

Care is all pervasive as a value and needs to be demonstrated every day. When people do not care, customer confidence collapses and companies crash. Care is not only having safe and reliable products that comply with regulatory standards, but is all about an attitude of mind that reflects genuine care.

All organizations have customers. If you don't care for your customers, then if they have a choice they will walk away. The people exercising that care on a day-to-day basis are your front-line staff. They are less likely to care if they sense that their team leader does not genuinely care for them.

Team leaders have to demonstrate every day that they care for both team members and customers. This means putting people before task and people before profit.

What a team leader cares about is always obvious to team members

Lyn Graham, head of internal audit at Portsmouth City Council, had a team member who came to work with a severe back problem. She sent him home and suggested that he work from there whenever he could. On his subsequent return to work, she discussed with him the purchase of a special chair to help him. Lyn cares and the team knows she does. They care too.

Showing that you care might be as simple as asking, "How is your wife? Is she getting better?" Or it might be approaching a team member who looks pale and tired and taking her aside to enquire about her wellbeing. It might mean devoting ten minutes and a sympathetic ear to someone who wants to tell you about a problem at home.

All your behavior will reflect the degree to which you care. When your team is busy doing the biz, care might mean fetching them coffee or making follow-up calls on their behalf.

To be caring requires a high degree of sensitivity over what is happening with your immediate team and their customers. Your antennae will pick up an alarm signal when you see certain things occurring. When Julie looks stressed and is running around "chasing her tail," that is the time to extend some care and provide support. When Jacques looks depressed after losing a sale, that is the time to put a metaphorical arm around his shoulder and provide encouragement.

Care is an emotional conduit between people's hearts. When you sense that someone is downhearted, you care for them by demonstrating empathy and by trying to lift their spirits. Care is a connection that leads to an increasing state of wellbeing, for the simple reason that you want people, customers, and team members alike to "feel good." Such care is reflected in a boss's everyday behavior.

THE BIZ STEP 31

Identify five different things you can do today to show that you genuinely care for the people in your team, together with five different things that show you also care for your customers.

BIZ POINT
Care is deep and it is final. Companies stand and
fall by the way they care for people.

MINIMIZE MEETINGS

To be available for team members, customers, and suppliers, team leaders must minimize time spent in meetings.

You can tell a badly run organization. Nobody is ever available. People are always in meetings. Furthermore, they are so busy (attending meetings) that it can take three months to get an appointment to see them. Everyone seems to get involved in everything.

Some employees struggle to get to see their bosses because they are always in meetings. This can be very damaging. Problems go unresolved and bosses lose touch with reality—all because of meetings. This invariably leads to a high degree of demotivation. The number of meetings should therefore be kept to a minimum.

No team leader should schedule their time so rigidly that there is no time to deal with the unforeseen problems and issues that inevitably arise on a daily basis. A rule of thumb is that the maximum amount of time scheduled for meetings in a manager's diary should be 25 percent, ideally less.

In restricting the number of meetings, the following minimal approach is suggested:

1 Daily team meetings, maximum 15 minutes, standing up. The sole purpose of these meetings should be to inform each other of what happened the previous day. There should be no discussion other than clarifications. Anyone can attend irrespective of status, department, and where they work.
2 Weekly team meetings, maximum half an hour, sitting down. The purpose of these meetings should be to review the previous week's performance and prepare for the forthcoming week.
3 Monthly team meetings, maximum three hours, sitting down. The purpose of these meetings should be to consider and decide on longer-term issues.
4 Two off-site retreats a year, one eight hours non-residential and the second twenty-four hours residential. The purpose of these is to review and develop strategies for the coming year.
5 Individual (one-to-one) face-to-face, one-hour sessions once a month for review of individual progress and discussion of individual issues.

Committees should be avoided like the plague, for the simple reason that they are normally devoid of individual accountability. The majority of committees are boring talk-shops where little listening goes on, even less understanding is created, and, what is worse, where few meaningful decisions are made. Even when decisions are made, the follow-through is inadequate. Committees find it difficult to hold an individual accountable for any action committed to in committee. So things do not get done when committees decide.

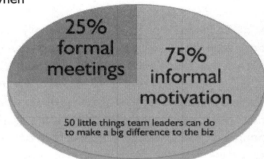

25% formal meetings

75% informal motivation

50 little things team leaders can do to make a big difference to the biz

Expressed another way, it is rare to find genuine commitment in a committee. Commitment is best found in teams with great leaders who hold themselves accountable for the contribution that they have agreed to make.

As a general rule of thumb, the companies that have the fewest committees and the fewest formal meetings are those that have the most motivated employees.

THE BIZ STEP 32

Be ruthless: Abolish all meetings that you personally consider are a waste of time.
Similarly, refuse to attend any meeting where your contribution will be minimal.

BIZ POINT
The more meetings a company has, the less individual accountability there is in that company.

32

33 MINIMIZE CONSULTATION

Only consult people as a last resort.

Some 90 percent of consultation is totally unnecessary. You can't have it both ways: You can either have consultation or you can have decisions, but you can't have both at the same time.

Consultation leads to delays, demotivation, and competitive decline. To do the biz you need team leaders who can make decisions and hold themselves accountable for them. It is a total waste of time to consult people on most decisions. People love bosses who make decisions—especially the right decisions, but then the best bosses tend to make the right decisions. Conversely, people hate bosses who never make decisions, who insist on the merry-go-round of consulting people left, right, and center.

The problem with too much consultation is that it fuzzes over a prime principle of doing the biz—and that is accountability. An organization can only thrive when all team leaders and all team members know exactly what contribution they are accountable for making. When you have that clarity of purpose, you just get on and do what needs to be done—and there's little need for consultation as a result. People are trusted to make the right decisions.

> "I am making a decision whether or not to consult you on the decision I should make, and that's whether or not I should consult you on the decision."

Another problem with consultation is that the amateurs try to advise the professionals, and the novices try to advise the experts. Every Tom, Dick, and Harry's opinion is given equal weight, when the person whose opinion should carry most weight is the person accountable for making the decision and implementing it.

Consultation is time-wasting, inefficient, and painfully frustrating, especially when it is clear what the decision should be. Even when it is not clear, someone has to be accountable for deciding on the risk. Often consultation drags on as people seek a consensus that never arrives. You can't please all of the people all of the time, so it is best to make an early decision and accept that you are going to upset some people as a result.

The only time to consult people is when you are unsure of your ground and need further information and advice. In these cases you are not ready to make a decision and consultation makes a lot of common sense.

Furthermore, when an issue is highly controversial it does make good sense to consult the vocal minority and allow them their say, taking their views into account if necessary. Sometimes expediency is preferable to absoluteness. A final reason for consulting people is if the potential decision has a major impact on their work.

Informing people of a decision is more important than consulting them on it

Team leaders who make decisions without consultation are not dictators, they are simply bosses who have the trust of their teams and their senior executives to do the biz in the desired direction. It is the bosses who lack confidence, clarity of purpose, and fitness of mind who hedge their bets by soliciting the views of the whole world.

The key is not in consultation but in informing people of your decisions. Thus you should never consult your boss on anything—for the simple reason that his or her view will become the decision. It is much more important to make your own decision, but then to have the courtesy of informing your boss what it is.

The Nike motto of "Just do it" is very apt for the biz.

THE BIZ STEP 33
Just do it. Make a decision and forget about consulting people—but do inform them of your decision.

BIZ POINT
Consultation is the death of decision making.

33

34 STAMP OUT BAD BEHAVIOR

Have a zero-tolerance approach to bad behavior.

Bad behavior demotivates all around. Nobody should be allowed to cross the line between good and bad behavior. Bad behavior is like a virus, infecting teams, draining them of energy, and causing immense damage. The weakest bosses fail to confront these problems and as a result a malaise sets in and performance deteriorates.

LINE OF ZERO TOLERANCE

Unacceptable	Acceptable
Bad behavior	Good behavior
Wrong side	Right side

Tolerable
blind eye
deaf ear
fringe zone

Each team leader will need to create in his or her mind a line of zero tolerance of behavior that is unacceptable and must be dealt with immediately if infringements occur. Close to the line will be certain fringe activities that the boss might not like but might well tolerate by turning a blind eye or deaf ear to them. Again, each leader will have to make a personal decision regarding what constitutes these fringe activities.

A few years ago I was speaking at a two-day residential conference in a hotel in Birmingham, UK. At 3.00 a.m. I was awoken by drunken delegates from another conference staggering along the corridor outside my room, shouting, singing, swearing, and banging on guests' doors. There were complaints to the hotel management, who dealt with the issue and in turn complained to the chief executive of the company employing the drunks. He was on site attending the conference. At 10.30 a.m. the culprits were called to a conference room and fired on the spot for bringing their employer into disrepute.

While mistakes can be tolerated, bad behavior cannot. It is corrosive and erodes the discipline necessary for a team to work well together in doing the biz and delivering results.

Further examples of bad behavior are when a team member:

- ✖ Runs other people down behind their back (and shows frequent disrespect for others).
- ✖ Is generally "difficult" (e.g., always raising objections when asked to do something).
- ✖ Makes offensive remarks about other people and/or makes rude gestures.
- ✖ Abuses privileges (e.g., uses company equipment for personal purposes).
- ✖ Utters racist, sexist, ageist, or any type of prejudicial remark.
- ✖ Swears, uses abusive language, shouts, and/or loses their temper.
- ✖ Is always late for meetings as well as for work.
- ✖ Frequently interrupts other people.
- ✖ Indulges in horseplay.
- ✖ Ignores people.
- ✖ Bullies someone.
- ✖ Fiddles expenses.
- ✖ Plays internal politics.
- ✖ Sexually harasses someone.
- ✖ Complains about everything.
- ✖ Does not listen to colleagues.
- ✖ Is more argumentative than cooperative.
- ✖ Steals company materials (e.g., stationery).
- ✖ Pins offensive pictures to walls and screens.
- ✖ Tells lies (or covers up, or does not come clean).
- ✖ Is always telling other people how to do their jobs.
- ✖ Spends a lot of time at work chatting about personal issues.
- ✖ Never volunteers for anything (leaving other team members to do the extra work).
- ✖ Fails to turn off their mobile during meetings and gives a higher priority to messages than to what colleagues are saying.

It's just not on!

THE BIZ STEP 34

Be proactive in preventing bad behavior. Work closely with your team to agree a code of conduct for how you work together. This need not be written down—but that does help. The code should be reviewed from time to time.

BIZ POINT
The root cause of poor performance is often bad behavior.

34

IMPROVING THE BIZ

The world moves on and we have to learn to move with it—if not ahead of it. Those who fail to improve fall behind and eventually fall off.

It is tough to be improving all the time, but it has to be all the time. Nobody can rely on an employer to provide all the set-piece improvement training necessary to get on. The reach of learning must be beyond the classroom: through everyday experiences, the media, the internet, books, and questioning the experts. Being motivated to continual improvement is the key, not the imposition of mandatory training.

35 TEACH YOURSELF

The best way to become an expert in doing the biz is to teach the subject. Turn yourself into a teacher.

Andrew Messenger, chief executive of the West Bromwich Building Society in the UK, makes it his top priority to attend every induction training program for new employees. For him people development (as he calls it) is top priority and he leads the way by contributing to the training program himself. He starts off the induction training with a talk, spends an hour or two with the trainees, and then joins them for lunch. The emphasis in his talk is on the Society's values and emphasis on people and customer service.

"My mind is in a class of its own!"

Nick Clayton, when he was general manager of the Ritz Carlton Hotel in Singapore, would personally undertake leadership training. Many executives from the hotel group conduct training sessions, including the CEO from time to time.

Jack Welch, former CEO of General Electric, stated that when GE was going through a tough period in the 1980s and had to lay off employees, the one thing he did not do was cut back on training budgets. In fact, he increased his investment at Crotonville, the company's management development center. "I loved teaching," he said and he would regularly contribute personally to programs at Crotonville.

So one little thing you can do as an enterprising team leader is to conduct the occasional training program on how to do the biz, not necessarily for your own team but for other teams too. This has many advantages. For a start, it forces you to develop and articulate your own expertise in motivation as well as to enhance your personal teaching skills. You can't stand up and run a session in front of a group of people unless you know what you are talking about and have the confidence to do so.

This means that you have to be on a continual learning curve yourself. There is always more to learn about doing the biz. If you are to teach the subject to others, whether by lecture or by facilitation, then first you have to teach it to yourself. You will be unlikely to be able to teach a group successfully about motivating people unless you have the wherewithal in motivation yourself. It does not happen by default. Teaching a subject therefore leads you to develop yourself.

Chris Hughes, previously with the Bradford & Bingley bank in the UK, invested substantial amounts in teaching himself. For example, he spent over £2,000 of his own money while with the bank to go and hear the American guru Anthony Robbins present a seminar. This personal learning helped put him ahead of the competition, benefited his customers, and contributed to his incredible success as a top performer.

When someone has a thirst for learning, their motivation will often be so great that they will want to pass on the valuable lessons to other people. An additional benefit of teaching others is that it subjects your thinking and approach to severe scrutiny. This can prove to be an invaluable test of your theories and practices. If there is any weakness in your argument, it will soon be exposed in a lively session.

THE BIZ STEP 35

Approach your training department and volunteer to run a motivation program for staff from other departments. If your company doesn't have a training department, arrange the session yourself.

BIZ POINT
What you learn about the biz is valuable.
Teach it so that others can benefit.

36 STUDY TEAM MEMBERS LIKE A BOOK

Study people. The more you do, the more you will understand and be able to deal with them.

We all have hidden complexities and even facets of our psychological makeup that we don't understand ourselves. It helps to have a team leader who seeks to understand. Those who fail to study people end up playing with figures and designing metalwork. The latter has to be done, but if you want to motivate people it is far better to study them than statistics and science.

It is worth quoting three women from Singapore on this subject. The first is Doris Chee, restaurant manager at the Oriental Hotel. She has it in a nutshell: "You have to study each team member like a book. You have to learn about an individual's strengths and weaknesses, about each person's character, motivations, skills and experiences, thoughts and feelings as well as the attitude and approach to the exceptionally high standards we set and expect. Only in that way can you help people learn and improve."

She goes on to say, "The more you know an individual the easier it is to deal with that person." The logic is irrefutable and it is therefore surprising that this subject is often so neglected.

Olivia Lum, founder and chief executive of the incredibly successful Hyflux Company, states: "I learnt early in life from my teachers that knowledge is power. I am therefore a very inquisitive person. I like to ask people lots of questions so I can understand what is going on and what is important."

The third woman is Nanz Chong-Komo, founder of the ONE.99 shop, who won the International Management Action Award in 2001. She comments, "I get insights into people's lives. Fifty percent of motivation is asking people how they are. Be interested in people first."

The best minute is the one you invest in learning about a particular person. In the absence of such study, misunderstandings are likely to arise and disasters occur as dissensions erode the fabric of morale in the organization.

The triggers for demotivation are frequently the little things that people say and do. Studying people therefore involves studying the small stuff: their microbehaviors, their subtle nuances of attitude, mood, body language, and eye movement. It means understanding each and every word and the meaning behind it, false or genuine. It means continually seeking answers to the question "Why?"—"Why did they behave like that?" or "Why did they say that?"

Such studies will reveal the reason behind the yawn, the bored look, the casual throwaway remark, and the automatic "No, it can't be done." They will help you understand why Jill always rushes to volunteer while Jack runs a mile to avoid taking any initiative. You will learn why Jane is always complaining and Jim is always cheerful.

Bosses who study people and seek understanding can help them change for the better, should they so want—and if people don't want to change, leaders can at least try to understand why they are sticking their heads in the sand and refusing to drink at the creek. Perhaps they fear non-existent crocodiles, or the crocodiles in their minds. In motivating people an excellent boss can help people wrestle with their fears and overcome them. But it takes a lot of study to do so. It involves listening and learning as opposed to telling and teaching.

The secret is to watch, observe, ask, explore, and build up pictures that reflect a person's total self: personality, positioning, and approach.

THE BIZ STEP 36
Each day focus on one member of your team, study him or her, and try to establish what makes this person tick. Learn from this and then help others learn too.

BIZ POINT
*The best bosses are an open book. Everyone
can read them and understand.*

36

37 DROP PEOPLE IN THE DEEP END

Help team members prove to themselves that they are capable of much more.

It is difficult to swim in shallow water. Furthermore, it is impossible to learn to swim by reading a textbook or attending classroom lectures. Learning to swim is all about pushing back the boundaries of your experience, being submerged, getting your head wet. It is also about eliminating some fairly deep-rooted fears and proving to yourself that most things are possible. The limits on achievement are mostly the limits that we artificially construct in our minds in order to protect ourselves.

The worst team leaders allow their people to paddle in shallow water every day. It is pleasant for a while, but ultimately it becomes boring. Meanwhile the competition has learnt to swim in the deep sea and has reached the other side of the bay.

Many people are happy to paddle through life and achieve little other than a degree of comfort—and such comfort can lead to complacency.

The best team leaders are aware that dropping team members in the deep end from time to time means that they are more likely to survive than if they remain protected in the shallow end. They will have a deeper experience of a wider range of issues and will be more able to cope with the pressures of intensifying competition. The deep-end experience provides many more valuable lessons than the shallow end.

Inevitably there is a high degree of risk in this deep-end experience. To learn effectively people must take risks and gain from pushing back boundaries. When risk is minimized the experience and learning are minimal—and consequently motivation erodes as people become entrenched in their attitudes and set in their ways. In contrast, dropping people in the deep end can prove highly motivational, as it sends a clear signal that the company believes in them and trusts them to take risky decisions. That's the biz.

Here are some examples of deep-end experiences into which team leaders can drop their people. A team member can be:

❖ Invited to present to the board (when normally the team leader does so).
❖ Asked to represent a director in important negotiations with a customer.
❖ Assigned the responsibility of organizing a major event (for example the company's ten-year anniversary celebrations).
❖ Asked to deputize for the boss who has been sent on a three-month assignment overseas.
❖ Given a six-figure budget and responsibility for a project to bring a new product to market.
❖ Asked to head up an important new company change initiative.
❖ Plucked out of nowhere and asked to be the chief executive's personal assistant for three months.
❖ Sent to take charge of the closure of a non-productive factory.
❖ Given two days' notice to pack and go overseas and hold the fort when a country manager is suddenly taken ill.

Effectively it means pushing as many people as possible to their limits—so that they can exceed them and become much more effective as a result.

Dropping people in the deep end is exciting and exhilarating and many people relish it. It can be like taking the highest bungee jump in the world. However, it is not for everyone and no matter how much a team leader passionately believes in giving people these phenomenal opportunities, there are always some who hold back, who will not take the risk and prefer to continue with the safety of the mundane. These people probably do not realize that in the long term they are putting themselves at risk, as with fewer skills and less experience they become less marketable than those who have been exposed to and taken advantage of the deep end.

THE BIZ STEP 37

Create some deep-end experiences for those members of your team who really have potential to excel in their career. For example, send them into the lion's cage to feed the top cats with some juicy information and proposals.

BIZ POINT
The depth of a person's mind is a function of their
willingness to take on deep-end experiences.

37

38 NURTURE

Take care to help each team member grow and develop.

It is the little tender touches that motivate people and help them grow. We are all more delicate than we make out. While we like to simulate thick skins to protect our self-esteem, most of us are sensitive to the nuances of other people's behavior, for example whether or not he spoke to us or ignored us, whether or not she took an interest in us as opposed to them, whether or not we were kept in the loop or left out.

Most times we don't let on. We don't reveal how we feel and the impact of other people's behavior on us. We attempt to conceal our limitations, vulnerabilities, and deficiencies. If exposed, we fear ridicule and lack of career progress. Yet paradoxically it is these very things that need exposure if we are to address them and develop.

This area is fraught with difficulty. It is very subjective and the exploration of someone's inner self has the potential to damage their ego. Through denial we hide from ourselves because there is a part of us that we want to hide from others—but it is this very part of ourselves that needs repair and regeneration.

In other words, we all need nurturing if we are to make progress along the rocky road of doing our best for the business. Those of us who are not nurtured either go wild with extreme behavior, oblivious to the impact on others, or shrivel up from lack of attention. If we are not nurtured we are unaware of ourselves and how others perceive us. We create an impression of what we want to be and delude ourselves that this is the impression others have of us. We accept their perception if it accords with our own self-image and dismiss it if it does not.

Such extreme unnurtured behavior encourages sycophancy, flattery, hypocrisy, and at its worst a dictatorial style of management. Nobody can tell unnurtured team leaders anything unless they want to hear it—and they only want to hear it if it conforms with their own version of events and their own heroic image of themselves.

Nurturing through coaching and counseling is the answer. In an ideal world everyone should have a mentor to whom they can turn in order to talk through the multitude of ambiguities, half-digested thoughts, worries, and fears that are inevitably inflicted on our delicate souls. We all need a confidant we can trust with our innermost thoughts and feelings—no matter how irrational and extreme they are.

The best bosses develop a fine sensibility that enables them to coach and counsel team members without fear of retribution if they reveal dark thoughts and extreme tendencies. The mere process of revelation can enable these thoughts and tendencies to be addressed—before they become too repressed and thus create the long-term potential for explosive impact. In this way each rose grows to be beautiful rather than being allowed to go wild and strangle others.

When team leaders run around in busy mode putting pressure on all and sundry, these vital opportunities for nurturing, coaching, and counseling pass them by. The long-term effect is an erosion of moral fabric in the organization. A decay sets in, with the consequent failure to nurture the fine souls who devote their energies to doing the biz.

Nurturing is a precious process with no immediate discernible benefit, but it is essential. None of us can exist alone. We all need another person to share our thoughts and help us work through them. With pressure our thinking becomes both muddy and muddled, with a resulting lapse in the quality of decision making. Managers need to demonstrate that they care by nurturing.

THE BIZ STEP 38

If you don't have one already, seek out a confidant who can help you develop and grow by listening to you and assisting you in straightening out your own crooked thinking.

Similarly, develop the skills of a confidant so that you can nurture at least one other person along the route to success.

BIZ POINT
Uncontrolled nature is wild, but with nurture it can grow to be beautiful.

38

39 SEND TEAM MEMBERS AWAY

Free up your people's minds. Ensure that they are periodically absent from the workplace.

The same old thing day in and day out breeds monotony, demotivation, and erosion in performance. People cannot contribute effectively if they are not occasionally freed from their regular routine. They begin to do things with their eyes shut and this can become dangerous.

If repetitive strain injury comes from tapping the keyboard for hours on end, repetitive brain injury also comes from processing the same old thoughts 100 times a day. Such are the scripted welcomes, the standardized questions, and the rehearsed responses. In the end this wears people out and no matter how much fun they have at work, they become exhausted with the exacting procedures and time-limited transactions that form part of their essential contribution. Instead of work being enjoyable and exciting, it becomes a chore that at times is difficult to face.

Such demotivated people absent themselves through sickness, real or simulated. They change jobs in the hope of new challenges and renewed interest.

The best team leaders don't allow their people to be worn out by the treadmill of everyday routine. They create temporary escape routes so that people can venture out and reenergize and improve themselves with new freedoms. As the cliché goes, "A change is as good as a rest."

The most highly prized form of absence from routine is an international trip. This frees up an individual to learn afresh and make an exciting new contribution. While it is expensive, foreign travel on an important project can prove to be a major investment in motivation. The benefit from company-sponsored international travel is immeasurable and everyone should be given the opportunity from time to time. It will broaden horizons and alter entrenched, institutionalized thinking. The company's culture will really buzz when people are given such opportunities. They will return with stories to tell that will whet their colleagues' motivational appetites.

Another valued form of absence is external training. Giving employees the freedom to be exposed to people from other companies as well as to experts expands their horizons.

Exchange visits can also be helpful. For example, head office staff should make field visits from time to time to experience reality. By the same token, field staff should visit head office to experience finality (this is where the buck stops).

Similarly, call center staff should be free occasionally to go and see the people who call them, to get to know what it feels like to be at the other end of the phone and the experiences that callers go through.

On a daily basis, this means taking a breath of fresh air, walking around the park with members of your team, or hopping over to Caffè Nero for a grand latte and a chat. Why not send your people to the pub for lunch on the last Friday of every week to brainstorm some great ideas?

Unless you send your people away they will turn into robots who mechanistically go through the same old routines every day. Everyone needs to be extracted from their environment from time to time and exposed to new ideas, thoughts, and practices.

THE BIZ STEP 39

Ensure that every team member is sent away from the workplace at least twice a year (in addition to their normal vacations). Plan it now and make it happen.

BIZ POINT
Even at work we need the freedom to be home and away.

39

THE SIX BIZ MINDSETS

The prime mindset for any effective team leader is to make people the top priority. However, there are a number of other interrelated mindsets that are required to support this approach and do the biz.

Perhaps 75 percent of a team leader's time, energy, and thinking should be devoted to people issues. The remaining 25 percent should be assigned to all the little things needed to apply the remaining five mindsets, all of which overlap to some degree.

FIRST MINDSET: PEOPLE

In doing the biz the first thing that should be on your mind is people.

On the very first day and during the very first hour after John Hayes took up his appointment as managing director of the John Lewis department store in Newcastle, UK, he was there at the partners' (employees') entrance to welcome everyone who worked in the store. He was thinking about his new team and he was there for them from that very first moment. He spent most of his first day on the shop floor, meeting people, listening carefully, and finding out what they thought.

Too many bosses are nowhere to be seen. They are distant. They spend their time in meetings, leaving front-line employees unaware of what is going on.

In fact, the only time you see some managers is when things go wrong—and then they are there to find fault, to criticize, to punish, and to instruct on a better way. These bosses always know a better way—after the event. They are driven by hindsight and specialize in reacting to the negative. They are experts in poor performance and the inevitable lapses in operational efficiency (which happen inevitably when they are not around).

The best team leaders "think people" all the time. They are conscious of the importance of team members and are therefore always considering different little ways to please them, help them improve their performance, and generally keep them motivated so that they go home at the end of the week with a sense of accomplishment.

"You are always on my mind"

What goes on in the minds of the best bosses is closely linked to the way they feel. They are emotionally intelligent and are conscious not only of the feelings of each team member but also of their own emotions. They are aware of the emotional dynamics in the team and the driving forces that propel their people forward.

In giving a great deal of time to the people side of the biz, good leaders focus their minds on effective communication. They know that the little things they say as bosses can make a big difference. So they give a lot of thought to the words they use, their tone of voice, and how best to give feedback. It is a two-way process, so they also give a lot of thought to what team members say to them. They are keen to listen to their ideas, conscious that they have a high regard for team members and trust them implicitly.

Give a little thought to your people today and every day

They will also spend hours thinking through the ins and outs of the type of people they should be hiring, the best training to give team members, and the most effective way of communicating with them.

Desperate for their people to succeed, these team leaders will apply a lot of mental energy to thinking about how best to support and help them in their endeavors.

Finally, they give a lot of thought to how to recognize and reward their people's hard work and the essentials they deliver. The last thing they want is for people to complain that they don't feel appreciated or valued.

THE BIZ STEP 40
Consciously devote time every day to thinking about the motivation of your team and what else you can do to foster it.

BIZ POINT
The best managers are there for their people.

40

41 SECOND MINDSET: CUSTOMERS

Motivate your people to build relationships with and understand customers, rather than sell to them.

As described in *The Buzz*, the companion book to this one, customers are the star performers of the business world. Customers are wonderful. Life would be so miserable without them. They score the goals for you, get your team to number one in the service league, and should be featured as icons of wise choice. Customers should be the light of our working lives. Without them our world would be dark—we would see nobody working. Without customers our world would be empty. There would be nothing to do. We wouldn't even be able to eat, let alone put a roof over our heads. Without customers we are nothing.

In doing the biz the key motivational message to reinforce in daily communications is that each team member is a "customer supporter" who helps customers achieve what they want in life by way of the purchases they desire and make. There is no more important cause than helping customers fulfill their dreams within your designated line of business. Every single employee's contribution should be focused on delivering this. Revenue and profit are a product of having happy people serving happy customers.

Charles Denton, managing director of Molton Brown, a progressive company that manufactures and retails skin-care products and toiletries, states, "We do not sell to customers, we assist them in making purchases."

The word "selling" has too many negative connotations, as if we are trying to persuade customers to buy something they are not convinced they want. Surely if they require these products they are going to buy them anyway? So there is no need for selling to them in the first place.

What is needed is to create an awareness among customers of your company's product offering and also to create an appetite for it. There are many little things that team leaders can do to help team members develop this creative approach.

For example, team leaders should enter the realms of psychology and explore the emotional interactions that take place when the team is "in touch" with its customers (whether they be internal or external). How do team members develop understandings with customers? How do they help establish customers' needs? How do they educate customers about the company's product line? Finally, what are all the the little things the team can do to create a customer buzz?

The answer to all these questions lies in the *art of question and suggestion* as opposed to the *pressure of persuasion*. These are fundamentally different and opposing mindsets.

The art of question and suggestion

The art of question and suggestion mindset requires you to place a lot of trust in customers to make decisions in your favor when it suits them. To achieve this a sensitive and engaging approach is needed, as opposed to an in-your-face, proactive, pushy approach. Each interaction should be aimed at relationship building and understanding needs, as opposed to traditional selling with its "closing the sale" techniques. It is only when customers indicate that they want to buy that a sale should be attempted, not before. Before this you should explore the customer's requirements and explain your product offering (given that the customer has sufficient interest to have chosen to be in the vicinity of these products).

THE BIZ STEP 41

Suggest to your team members that they stop thinking about selling and instead focus solely on building relationships with customers (internal and external), understanding their needs and how these can best be met.

BIZ POINT
All teams should keep in mind that customers are their raison d'être.

41

42 THIRD MINDSET: MONEY

Spend five minutes a week worrying about money, no more.

One chief executive (who had better be nameless) told me, "Money is boring. I leave it to the accountants to sort out. I spend all my time with my employees and my customers. That's where I do the biz and that's how I get the buzz!"

Regrettably, money has become an obsession in many companies, especially with regard to cost cutting. As we all know money (let alone cost cutting) does not bring happiness in an organization. What does is a growing number of satisfied customers served by motivated and high-performing people. Revenue, profit, and shareholder value are the important by-products. This is the critical "money mindset" for doing the biz.

In developing this mindset it is important to differentiate between "bad" costs and "good" costs. Bad costs lead to inefficiency, poor service, and low quality, and therefore should be eliminated.

Good costs, in contrast, bring value to the business in terms of efficiency, customer satisfaction, quality, and morale. This in turns leads to revenue generation. Sadly, too many organizations fail to differentiate between the two and thus cut back on good costs to the detriment of the customer and the business.

For example, there is an international five-star hotel chain where staff used to provide a complimentary bottle of mineral water by the guest's bedside. Now they don't. Management has cut down on the toiletries too—there are no longer bottles of hair conditioner in the bathroom. Nor do they put chocolates on the pillow. In the lounge they used to put paper coasters under the cocktail glasses as they served the drinks, but they have stopped doing this. They also used to put a vase and flowers on each table; no longer. The furniture has begun to look tatty and needs refurbishing, but has not been renewed. Customers notice all these little details and slowly

Money is boring! It's what people do with it that's exciting

move their business to competitors. The occupancy levels and yields of this hotel chain are down.

There is an airline that used to do wonderful little things like serve economy-class passengers juice or water before take-off and then provide printed menus before the meal. They would also offer ice creams mid-flight. They no longer do any of this. Again, customers notice and when given a choice will transfer their allegiance to different airlines that provide a better service for the same price. Similar stories can be told of banks and companies in many other industries.

Good costs
_____ ✓
_____ ✓
_____ ✓

Bad costs
_____ ✗
_____ ✗
_____ ✗

Doing the biz requires a money mindset in which investments can be made to secure maximum customer satisfaction and the highest levels of employee morale and performance. Every item of expenditure should beg the question: "Does this cost bring value to the company in terms of efficiency, customer satisfaction, quality, and morale?" If the answer is "yes," then it can be designated a good cost. If the answer is "no," then the money should not be spent and the cost can be eliminated.

To motivate your team members all you need to do is give them the authority to make decisions on good costs, provided that they are within budget. This follows a key principle of this book, trust, as discussed in Chapter 7.

THE BIZ STEP 42
Reexamine your budget and discuss with your team the difference between good costs and bad costs, producing as many examples of each as possible. Which category does traveling business class fall into, for example?

BIZ POINT
The money mindset is equivalent to the mindset of "value for money." That's value for the customer and the business.

42

43 FOURTH MINDSET: POSITIVITY

Create a "can do" attitude by converting negatives into positives and always saying "yes" to team members.

An alternative term for positivity is "can do." Analogous to this is being constructive, optimistic, and confident as well as affirmative. Nothing is too much trouble for team leaders who are positive and they will do every little thing possible to help.

This "yes" mindset has already been mentioned in Chapter 28 and is highly motivating. Team leaders with positive mindsets create mental barriers that prevent any negative event dragging them into emotional states of anger and misery. As soon as anything goes wrong, they erect barriers in their minds to stop them slipping into "moan mode" and projecting the problem onto others.

Team leaders with a positive mindset never suffer from the "blame syndrome" and never have a stack of excuses in their back pocket ready to explain mistakes, failures, and setbacks. Instead, they tend to be full of passion and belief as well as sufficiently humble and excited to know that there is much more to learn. They do not dwell on their own limitations but seek to remove them in achieving what they want out of life and work. These are the bosses who set their sights high, wanting to push back the boundaries rather than confine themselves to the comfort and security of the status quo and the monotony of everyday routine.

These people tend to focus on the positive things in life as opposed to the negative. We live in a highly imperfect world and it is unlikely that we will achieve perfection, paradise, or utopia next week. Therefore to remain happy we have to accept many imperfections and limitations. Positive people don't allow these negatives to defeat them but use each as a spur to greater success. They know that you can't experience success without failure. So when things go wrong and they experience setbacks, they don't give up.

When motivating people these positive team leaders search for the good in people and only focus on the negative when it can be used as an agreed spur for improvement. They choose to look for the fine qualities that most people have and try to help them develop these further, building on their strengths while minimizing their weaknesses. In seeking out the good these bosses tend to find things in people they like rather than things they dislike. As a result, they are full of positive comments and helpful suggestions. They are reluctant to criticize and only do so when they sense that the recipient will welcome it as helpful.

Most importantly, when motivating people these positive bosses are always reluctant to say "no." They seek wherever possible to say "yes" to suggestions or requests. Their essential approach is "can do." Very rarely do they say "can't do."

There is a chain of hairdressing salons in Taiwan called Mentor that prints a little booklet for front-line employees suggesting all the things they can do for their customers. For example, they can teach customers about new hairstyles and new shampoos and products coming onto the market. They can chat to them and build relationships with them. Essentially, the philosophy of the company is a "can do" one, based on a mindset of positivity. Not specified is what employees can't do.

Karmjit Singh, a senior executive with Singapore Airlines Terminal Services (SATS), initiated a "yes" campaign that has been going on for over five years and is now into its fifth strategic phase. The essence of the approach is to say "yes" to exceptional service and for employees on the ground at Changi Airport to initiate positive action to help customers.

THE BIZ STEP 43
Have a "yes" day. Say "yes" to every request and suggestion that comes to you.
Then go out and look for positives in your team members and highlight them.

BIZ POINT
"No" is the most demotivating word in the English language. The most motivating word is "yes."

FIFTH MINDSET: 110% ATTITUDE

Go beyond the norm, give extra.

To do the biz you cannot afford to be selfish. You cannot always be on the take, expecting more for less. In fact, to deliver the greatest results you have to give more than you take.

The key word is sacrifice. Nothing can be achieved without a front-end sacrifice. For example, you cannot complete a marathon within your target time unless you train for months on end and sacrifice many off-duty hours to running around parks and along miles of streets. Nor can you achieve world-class customer service unless you sacrifice precious time and resources in training your people to deliver it.

Sacrifice is an investment of your time, energy, and resources. It means stretching yourself to give more than you think you have, but with the confidence that there will probably be a return at the end of the day.

In customer service circles this is called "going the extra mile" (nobody ever says "going the extra kilometer"!).

A 110% attitude means:

✛ Putting nine hours of your time in when the contract specifies eight.
✛ Sparing no effort and time to help a team member resolve a protracted problem.
✛ Dipping into your own pocket to buy drinks for your team when other people are too mean to buy them.
✛ All the additional things you do for your customers, for example waiving a delivery charge on a special occasion.
✛ Volunteering a discount on the tenth occasion a customer makes a purchase.
✛ Presenting a high-performing team member with a specially selected gift.
✛ Dropping what you want to do and doing something requested by someone else.
✛ Not charging your full expenses.
✛ Working over the weekend to complete a project.
✛ Focusing all your energies on a key customer and not allowing yourself to be distracted.

The 110% attitude is critically important in motivating team members. They will know that team leaders will really put themselves out to help them with their everyday work as well as spare no expense in digging them out of a hole. Good team leaders will stay until 6.30 p.m. for a team member who urgently wants to see them, rather than go home at 5.30 p.m. as planned. They will even come in at 3.00 a.m. if need be.

Such bosses are unstinting in their efforts to motivate team members to do the biz and furthermore will stop at nothing to please customers. Their personal comfort and wellbeing are far less important than the welfare of the people they support and serve on an everyday basis. They never complain when they have to give up time or spend their own money on addressing an issue.

Always err on the right side of giving 100%

X ✓

90   100   110

Overall, they set their sights on achieving more than the 100% norm. They know that many people do the minimum necessary to deliver the minimum required of them. By putting in extra effort, these 110% bosses put themselves at a competitive advantage, aware that they are likely to deliver better results than those who only apply minimal effort. By putting more into their customers they achieve better levels of customer satisfaction. By putting more into their team members they achieve higher levels of motivation and morale.

The 110% attitude is infectious. When team members see bosses giving everything possible there is to give, they will be prepared to do the same when the chips are down and a superlative result is required.

THE BIZ STEP 44
Ask yourself whether you have a 90%, 100%, or 110% attitude as far as your job as team leader is concerned.

BIZ POINT
If you don't give 110% then someone else will and they will be ahead of you.

44

45 SIXTH MINDSET: GO M.A.D.

Don't be the same as every other manager, become a pioneer for the biz. Make a difference!

Nothing stays still. Nothing remains the same as before. The status quo and emulation of practices by past masters will not take you to a bright future. Expressed another way, unless you devote a little time every week to finding a better way, then one of your competitors will and you will be second best.

To achieve this requires the ability to challenge virtually everything that goes on in the organization by periodically asking yourself and your team the simple question: "Is this the best and only way? Can't we find a better or different way?"

Is this the best/only:

- ❖ Product (range) we have? Can't we find a better/different product (range)?
- ❖ Way to serve our customers? Can't we find a better/different way?
- ❖ Way to operate? Can't we find a better/different way?
- ❖ Way to manage the business? Can't we find a better/different way?
- ❖ Way to motivate employees? Can't we find a better/different way?
- ❖ Way to market our products and services? Is there a better/different way?
- ❖ Way to do the biz? Is there a better/different way?
- ❖ etc., etc.

There always is a better or different way. Companies like Starbucks and Ryanair, which did not exist in the 1980s, have found their own way. Change is of the essence and the best team leaders are always on the lookout for new ideas and keep an open mind to all possibilities that come across their path. They then exploit them by pioneering a new approach.

They seek these ideas from their team members as well as under-taking research into what other people in the world are doing in order to stimulate their own ideas. They are prepared to take risks by investing time and money to support their teams in pursuing these innovative new concepts. As a result, they encourage creativity and experimentation. This proves highly motivational.

For example, a taxi driver in South Africa pioneered a new approach by offering passengers he collected at Johannesburg Airport complimentary juices and mineral water from an ice box, while another taxi driver in New York presented his passengers with a menu of music they could choose from depending on whether they liked jazz, classics, pop, or silence.

Be M.A.D.
Make A Difference

The opportunities for pioneering a new approach are endless. At the European headquarters of Nike in Hilversum, employees choose their own working hours, when to take breaks, where to hold meetings, and where to do their work.

Happy Computers has pioneered the approach of offering ice creams at 4.00 p.m. every day to everyone on its premises at Adler Street in London, whether they be customers, employees, van drivers, security guards, or visitors. It also encourages its employees to devote time during working hours to helping charities.

Doing the biz means looking for new ideas all the time and then pioneering the most attractive ones. It means being a little bit M.A.D. every day.

THE BIZ STEP 45

Set yourself a personal objective of pioneering one new idea—either suggested by a team member or something you have come up with yourself—over the next month.

BIZ POINT
Go MAD. Make.A.Difference.
Become a pioneer.

45

THE FINAL FIVE

All the best bosses I have ever had have been a little eccentric or, as mentioned in the previous section, a little M.A.D. They exhibited some endearing features that were mighty unusual but that people liked and got them talking. One boss would wear socks that were either bright red or bright yellow. On one occasion he wore one of each. On another occasion he came to work wearing one brown shoe and one black shoe. He had got up early and dressed in the dark, not turning on the light for fear of disturbing his wife.

Another boss was exceptionally indiscreet, but we loved him for it. His utterances certainly enlivened our days and stimulated much coffee-time talk. He loved to quote a very famous chairman who used to tell his son (who was in the business), "How many more times do I have to fire you before you do what you are told?"

To excel at motivation and be a great team leader, it helps to have a colorful personality, which includes a number of distinctive idiosyncrasies and of course signs of minor madness.

46 BE INDISCREET

While discretion might be the better part of valor, indiscretion is one of the better parts of motivation. It is better to be a little indiscreet than too discreet.

The world turns on gossip, scandal, hearsay, rumor, and titbits of fascinating information. Official statements are rarely motivating. In a free society the media is full of speculations, unsubstantiated facts, and assertions that stimulate social intercourse.

Being indiscreet means giving something away that officially you should not. It means revealing a spicy little detail that your elders would prefer to be kept hidden.

Indiscretion is a declaration of trust. It effectively says, "I will take you into my innermost sanctum and trust you with a thought, a feeling, or a confidence that I would not reveal to you if I did not trust you."

Team leaders who are too discreet close themselves off from their people, most of whom love to sit around and chat about what is happening at work. These managers come across as aloof and not one of the team. In their reluctance to expose themselves they seem distant, even pious, as well as driven by denial of the obvious: that formality in communication never fascinates people.

Informality is a key to motivation in that it frees up people's thinking and behavior as opposed to the formal restrictions of propaganda, programmed minds, and disciplined behavior. Informality thus requires a swirl of interchange between people as they allow a free flow of thinking to be injected into the essential socialization process. This kind of informality can take place in a formal meeting as well as in impromptu encounters.

MOTIVATIONAL INDISCRETION

"This is in total confidence..."

"I have been sworn to secrecy, so promise you won't tell anybody else..."

"If I can let you into a secret..."

"I am not supposed to tell you this, but..."

"This is for your ears only..."

Debate, democracy, and freedom of discussion are messy. They can't be restricted to the clean lines of official talk. As we all know, a little dirt is good for us and in environments that are clinically clean and wholesome there tends to be a lack of soul. An indiscretion is that little piece of dirt that keeps us alive, fresh, and well—and prevents us being turned into robots, programmed to think and behave exactly as our masters require.

There are unspoken rules, of course. The indiscretion should never be malicious, never knowingly deceitful let alone vindictive. Its purpose is to keep people fresh, so that they are completely up-to-date with the unofficial news ahead of the boring official statements.

Indiscretion not only relates to restricted facts but also to comment and the boss's unrestricted thinking. A team will always relish the opinion of their boss, for example when he meets a new senior executive they will want to know his opinion: "To be honest, I found her a bit pompous and too full of herself—a bit like me really!"

Good team leaders use indiscretions wisely to motivate their team. They take them into their confidence and whet their appetite for work with little titbits that they are not entitled to. It puts them ahead of the game and gives them the status of being in the know. It puts bosses at risk because if they are found out releasing confidential information or expressing opinions about a person behind their back, they will be in trouble. It happens: that is the risk. But it is a risk worth taking.

Finally, the indiscretion should always relate to what is happening in other parts of the organization. When a change affects an individual the first person to hear should always be that individual. No one else.

THE BIZ STEP 46
Find out what your team members want to know and then tell them, even if it means being a little indiscreet.

BIZ POINT
Indiscretion is a function of trust. The more you trust a person, the more indiscreet you can be.

46

LOOK HAPPY

Take a look at what makes you happy at work and then look happy.

A good reflection of motivation is a happy look on someone's face, especially a team leader. It is one little thing they can do every day: look happy.

Look happy:
- ☺ Coming to work
- ☺ Greeting customers
- ☺ Seeing team members
- ☺ When starting team meetings
- ☺ When asked to help with a problem
- ☺ Showing a director around your office
- ☺ When team members have exciting news to tell you
- ☺ When team members make a positive contribution

Happiness is a reflection of a positive spirit. It is a choice, but not everyone makes it for the simple reason that they are unaware they have this choice. Therefore they react instinctively to events and the behavior of other people. They see something funny and they instinctively laugh, which makes them happy. Or something goes wrong and they instinctively frown because they are unhappy.

Rachel, an executive officer working for a government agency, tells of

Happiness is a choice

her boss Jenny, the head of department: "Jenny is one of these people who has severe mood swings. Most mornings she comes in and is bright and bubbly. She just breezes through the day. As a result we feel good and we are bright, bubbly, and breezy too. On some occasions however she is called up to meet her senior executive and comes out of his office an hour or so later eyes down and with a long drawn-out face, full of woe. We know instantly that she is in a bad mood and that she will snap at us if we say anything. So we avoid her and go about our work with our tails between our legs."

For most people happiness (and conversely unhappiness) is infectious. One person's mood can have a major impact on another. Richard, a personnel manager in a company distributing industrial cleaning agents, confides, "When I go home in the evening I only have to open the door and see the look on my wife's face to know what mood she is in. The same when I telephone her, the tone of her voice in answering the call tells me everything. It can relax me or it can put me on my guard."

Peter, a middle manager with a transport company, says, "If you want a favor from our boss, for example an unscheduled day off, you have to wait until he's in the right mood to approach him. If you pick a bad day he will never give you the decision you want."

Most people are totally unaware of the impact of their moods on others, let alone on others. They are not even aware sometimes that they are in a bad mood. Bad spirits are often deceptive.

One of the skills in motivating people is therefore to develop a high degree of self-awareness and to that extent to choose positive, happy moods that radiate across to others. This is relatively easy to do. All it requires is for you to go looking for the good things in life that make you happy. Believe it or not, there are enough of these good things around that if you go looking for them you will find them. Conversely, if you focus solely on the negative, on problems, on bad behavior and things that go wrong, you will be in a permanent state of misery. As a result, your face will show it and this will have a deleterious impact on your team.

The key is to wake up every morning and consciously identify some aspect of your forthcoming day at work that you are looking forward to. Happiness and motivation then become a self-fulfilling prophecy as everyone begins to look on the bright side. This can even be done in times of adversity. After all, it can only get better. That's the spirit!

THE BIZ STEP 47
Undertake a happiness audit. Just ask people to answer truthfully: "Are you happy at work?" It is imperative that you address any issues they identify that make them unhappy.

BIZ POINT
Where there is hope there can always be happiness. This principle applies until the moment you die.

111

48 BE UNHAPPY FROM TIME TO TIME

Do a reality check and dose yourself up with unhappiness once in a while.

Unhappiness coexists with happiness. Be happy that the jug is half full. Be unhappy that the jug is half empty. Be happy that your team has improved its performance. Be unhappy that it is still not consistently the best.

Too much happiness can lead to complacency, arrogance, hubris, and cerebral blindness. Happiness is like a drug—it can obviously make you feel good, but too much of a good thing is bad for you. While it is great to be positive all the time, there is a risk that this will blind you to all the negatives in life. Surfing on the crest of a happiness wave can never be permanent. All waves have to die out sooner or later.

To make progress in life you need occasionally to come off the happiness drug and feel the pain of imperfection. In this way you can deal with unhappiness more effectively than pretending that everything is sunshine and roses.

The lesson is clear. Don't delude yourself in any circumstance that everything is fine. It never will be. We don't live in that type of world; instead, we live in one that we have already noted is imperfect. This applies at work too. The key to improvement is to identify the imperfections that make customers, shareholders, and of course employees unhappy. Identification of unhappiness factors (positive thinkers call them challenges) is essential for improvement and progress.

Happiness and unhappiness are therefore two sides of the same coin. You can be unhappy that you have not won the contract because Jimmy screwed up on the estimate, but you can also be happy that you have learnt a lesson and that a new challenge now awaits you (and Jimmy). Positive thinking requires that every negative be turned into a positive—but this does not mean that negatives do not exist. They do and they should be a cause of unhappiness to you.

PERFECTION — 100

Unhappiness — x

Happiness — y

Of course you should be unhappy about Jack's behavior at Jill's farewell last evening. Of course you should be unhappy that your boss neglected to tell you about the latest organizational change, especially when your team had discovered it before you. Of course you should be unhappy with yourself for missing an opportunity to pacify a customer who has now taken his business elsewhere.

As a boss, if you are not unhappy some of the time then you must be a freak. It is impossible (unless there is something seriously wrong with you) to go round looking happy all the time. Your team will think you live in a different world.

PERFECTION	100
Unhappiness	(x)
IDENTIFY THE UNHAPPINESS FACTORS	
Happiness	y

While you choose to be happy with all the good things you can identify at work, you should also choose, on rare occasions, to be unhappy with all the imperfections that you and your team need to address. It is a matter of choosing when to express happiness and when to express unhappiness in motivating your team. At the appropriate moment, each can be effective.

Some employees accuse their bosses of never being satisfied while others are accused of being too satisfied with the status quo. It is a balancing act and thus a personal choice to attain a motivational equilibrium between happiness and unhappiness.

A rare dose of healthy unhappiness can do your team a world of good. It's a bitter spirit.

THE BIZ STEP 48
Undertake an unhappiness audit. Just ask people to answer truthfully: "Are you unhappy at work?" It is imperative that you address any issues they identify that make them unhappy.

BIZ POINT
Unhappiness can be a fantastic motivator.
Trade on it once in a while.

49 EXPERIMENT WITH NEW MOTIVATIONAL STIMULI

Stimulate your team's motivation with one small experiment.

The enemies of the biz are repetition, prescription, routine, pursuit of the obvious, and the unquestioned application of previously defined best practice (now designated as policy and procedure).

As we have seen throughout this book, no longer are people motivated by doing the same old thing day in and day out. Nor are they content to be motivated in the same way as people were 50 years ago. People are now exposed to a wide variety of stimuli and unless a boss experiments with new motivational stimuli, there is a risk of a motivational loss, as indicated in the diagram below.

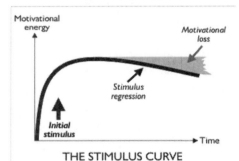

THE STIMULUS CURVE

It is well known that a single motivational stimulus (such as a pay increase) will only have a temporary effect. Initially the award of a pay increase will put the person on a motivational high. Then as time progresses the motivational effect wears off and fresh stimuli are required to prevent the individual becoming tired and jaded, leading to motivational loss. The same applies to any other motivational stimulus, whether it be a team picnic, a quiz or game, or some exciting training course. The motivational impact is far from permanent.

Team leaders who are effective in motivating their teams have very much an experimental style. They are always trying out new ideas and fresh stimuli to keep their teams on a high and perform effectively in doing the biz. This is illustrated in the following diagram:

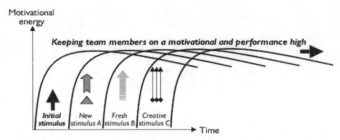

THE STIMULUS EFFECT

Below are just a few little ideas you can experiment with to stimulate your team's motivation:

- ✔ Encourage your people to devote a little time at work to a charitable cause or to community work.
- ✔ Experiment with a new dress code (everyone to wear something yellow on a Thursday).
- ✔ Experiment with a new series of learning workshops facilitated by a lecturer from the local college.
- ✔ Experiment with theme days, for example a Thai day when everyone brings in something related to Thailand.
- ✔ Experiment with games, quizzes, and competitions to increase product knowledge.
- ✔ Experiment with a "word of the day," choosing a different word every day. Monday's might be "listen" (we focus on listening to customers and colleagues); Tuesday's might be "special" (we focus on doing something special for people); Wednesday's might be "smile" (we focus on smiling at everyone we encounter that day); Thursday's might be "curiosity" (we focus on asking people questions and learning something new about them); and Friday's might be "hospitality" (we focus on being hospitable to people by offering tea, coffee, etc.).

Developing an experimental style of motivation will encourage team members also to be creative in coming up with new ideas. This in itself will be motivational.

THE BIZ STEP 49
Risk experimenting with just one new idea to motivate your team.
It could even be a "no swearing" day, with penalties for people who don't comply.

BIZ POINT
Motivation has to be stimulated with experimental ideas.

49

50 RETREAT, RELAX, REFLECT, REVIEW, AND RECHARGE

Take time out to retreat, relax, and reflect on the motivation of your team, what they are achieving, and where they are going.

The hard work has to stop some time. Then there is a need to retreat, relax, reflect on events, review possibilities, and recharge your batteries.

Good team leaders don't burn themselves out by sustaining a frenetic pace and being busy for extended periods. This can be highly demotivating for a team. Bosses who never stop tend to drive a team crazy.

The danger is that we lose sight of what it is all about as we chase our tails responding to the maelstrom of interruptions, emails, calls on the mobile, planned and unplanned meetings (and that is before the paperwork begins). For many people there is simply too much going on to find the time to sit back and reflect. But this is what we must do—and the best bosses do it. Failure to do so brings the inherent danger of myopia, of losing perspective and not being able to see the picture for the pixels. We lose sight of the objective and the contribution we are there to make for the company.

We think in patterns and unless we devote time to allowing pictures to emerge we will have no basis on which to place some shape and form on current events and the hard work we are putting in. We will experience individual events without realizing their significance and their place in the overall trend of things to come.

So take a walk in the park every day to allow fresh air to flow through your mind and flush away immediate thoughts. This will replenish your mental energies and bring exciting new perspectives. They will definitely emerge if you allow time and this will be highly motivational for your team. When you are busy and stressed, your peripheral vision suffers and all you can see is the narrow object in front of you. To obtain the big picture, past, present, and future, it is essential that you relax your mental muscles and allow some cerebral massaging to take place. Green trees, beautiful flowers, lakes, rivers, and eye-catching sculpture and architecture can provide the stimulus for a fresh flow of thoughts. Break off from your hard work and devote half an hour every day to such relaxed thinking.

Then once in a while, perhaps on a quarterly basis, escape from your everyday location to some distant, fertile pasture where you can obtain an even longer-term perspective. Vacations are a great help here, as also are two-day retreats with your team and other groups of interested parties. Residential workshops and seminars can usefully serve this purpose.

In retreating to reflect and recharge, it is important that you review your team's motivation. Examine your own approach and question whether you have allowed yourself to drift into routine and habit and have thus become too predictable, too undemanding, and insufficiently experimental and challenging.

Try to reach out and grab any exciting ideas that bubble through the creative cauldron of your recharged mind. Explore these ideas avidly and resist the temptation of instant rejection, of "can't do it because I haven't done it before." Return from the retreat prepared to be different—but not to such a degree that your team will not recognize you (this would not be credible). It might just be that you come to work without a tie when you have always worn a tie, or you come to work wearing a suit when your team has rarely seen you out of jeans. Every little change you make will have a motivational impact, for the simple reason that the change, whatever it might be, will stimulate debate and interest and will thus start channeling your team's energies in different and perhaps more exciting directions.

THE BIZ STEP 50
Stop everything and go for a walk. Just tell people that you are going to get some fresh air. Encourage your people to do the same. Then every three or four months organize a retreat for a couple of days with your team to reflect on doing the biz: now, then, and in the future.

BIZ POINT
To restore full power you need to recharge your mental, emotional, and spiritual batteries.